Delicate Torture

Delicate Torture

✦

(Living Poetically)

Kanaan

iUniverse, Inc.
New York Lincoln Shanghai

Delicate Torture
(Living Poetically)

iUniverse, Inc.

For information address:
iUniverse, Inc.
2021 Pine Lake Road, Suite 100
Lincoln, NE 68512
www.iuniverse.com

ISBN: 0-595-30384-6

Printed in the United States of America

Contents

To the reader,

...maybe this contradicts your idea of what a "professional" writer would do...(and my advisors think I'm **insane**) but I never considered myself a "professional" anything...(or sane for that matter) and I think labels like that remove us from each other in ways that are unimportant and counterproductive...and even though I have a so-called Master's Degree, I do not think that my education makes me any more qualified to be **great** than anyone else...I have included many poems here, they are all distinct stories, each with a different message, but all dedicated to you dear reader...take what you want, and leave the rest. There will be those of you who really get what I'm trying to say, you will understand innately because these truths are within you too, **you will be inspired, and renewed, and compelled to do something of profound beauty**, and for that I am grateful...for that I live and eagerly anticipate your response...for you I have written my soul out as best as I could so that you could read every syllable of silly tragic me...you may not agree with everything I have to say, but that's to be expected, you will at least see that there is beauty being born here...on the other hand, *if you skim through any of my books haphazardly you're sure to be offended, think me vain, or feel attacked in some way,* **I've been told that my existence disturbs some people...**but if you really give my books their due, honestly approaching them with **an open mind**, you will see that I am driven, sincere, passionate and genuinely concerned about and interested in you. **For me poetry is a delicate torture, it "kills me softly" as the saying goes...every poem that I have ever written has been based on real life, real people, real moments that were lived and are living still...they have been heartfelt and sincere...I hope you feel that when you read them.** I just have something that my soul is compelling me to say, I just wanna give something of beauty and significance back to the universe for all that it has given me...**I have two choices with my books, be honest and real, or be commercial and fake, I chose honesty.** So try not to judge me too harshly "lest you be judged like wise" (as the saying goes) but keep an open spirit, and perhaps you will be enlightened, and perhaps not, either way...you and I will be connected, and the world will be that much better off for having shared itself. I am a teacher, **an imperfect prophet** of things to come...and I want to know YOU, and I want you to know that I am serious about wanting to change the world for the better, and you dear reader are a big part of that equation, I cannot do it without you...help me! **Help me make the world a better place!** Together WE can do all things. Most authors are out of reach...but not me, I want to be a real person, and I want to do something few other artists have done before, by being available to my audience...**I want to do something profound before it's too late**...to accomplish this, I need to be connected to you dear reader...and so if this book speaks to you in any way then check out my first book called **Literati** (A Revolution of Living), my second trilogy called: **The Comma Sutra** (Turning?'s into!'s) my celebrated book called: **The Anatomy of a Moment** (An Intimate Portrait of Things Unseen) and the many more life changing books which are to follow...or feel free to contact me at: DelicateTorture@msn.com or call me at **714-317-POET** to let me know if I have touched you. I am a real person, as are you, and together...we can change everything as we know it!!!

Poetically,
Kanaan

DELICATE TORTURE

I have written the universe on a single sheet of paper
like so many sentences that will be misunderstood
by the time I am done.
And of all the words that have delighted me along the way,
none hung from my lips as sweet as your name.
I wonder if you will ever truly know
how much I have loved and been in love with you…
how much I have needed and cherished you,
how much my soul has begged me to belong to you…
what a delicate torture you are.
You are like delicious tiny raindrops
tickling down my spine.
You fascinate me.
One day you will read and reread this poem
in an effort to remember what true love is all about,
so let me remind you now…
Its about never letting go,
its about 3am night kisses
that leave you sleepy and smiling,
its about being aware of every moment,
even the tiny do nothings that decorate the day.
Its about mistakes and hopeful hugs,
its about never being ashamed…
and its about forgiving,
above all…forgiving.
Its about held hands
that always leave you wanting more…
Its about you and me,

being together somehow in this crazy mad world…
being together…
because we could not stand
to be without.

AS BEAUTIFUL AS YOU

Let it be said that I poured all my soul into this page...
let there be a remembrance of the poems I created in honor of you,
let the world hear something of beauty
in the way I have spelled out your smile...
let them breathe in deep
with their eyes closed and their minds open...
Let them say that this poet managed to recreate the world
in the image of his beloved
and in the years to come,
when lovers are looking for the words to express their connections...
let this serve as a scripture from which to find inspiration,
let the sincerity of these dreams wash over them...
like only poetry can,
let the universe know that people still fall madly in love
with reckless abandon
and that passion is still thrown to the wind in the name of desire.
let people everywhere begin to follow our example,
let them begin to make choices that are politically incorrect,
choices that are made by the heart,
choices that defy logic...
let them kiss, and embrace, and never let go,
let all the souls seeking completion,
come to our table they are welcome here...without judgment,
let their arms unfold with longing...
let them find peace in the eyes of a stranger...
Let them know belonging at last...
the kind of belonging I have found in you,
the kind that redeems, and heals, and forgives...
and when all has been said and done,
in the end...

let the world be saved by a poem as beautiful as this,
as beautiful as you.

OURS ALONE

Sounds fantastic, but last night I bent steel with just my bare hands,
together we watched stars fall from their cradle in the sky…
and then fell asleep above the canopy of clouds that carpeted our dreams…
I remember carrying everything I owned on my back
bags clung to me like children too young to walk on their own,
and laughing wildly with you in the sunshine beside the road.
Look how far we've come,
from a distance that can't be measured in miles,
and yet crossing the ocean was the tiniest of our difficulties,
we seemed to float there on gossamer wings made of sincerity…
Searching the night sky for satellites was the greater achievement…
how we oohed an aahed at their passings,
such marvels to preoccupy our time…
And making love in the Martian night,
while the red planet hung low for all to see,
we snuck high to escape their sight.
How blessed am I to have known your womb and all its delights,
and greater still is the tenderness of your kiss…
it is a secret which I relish to my soul's satisfaction.
Let the sway of these trees be my words,
let the wind carry them to you,
and deliver them to your cheek…
let your pillow be my chest,
and find some comfort there between my shoulders.
One day I will take you beyond those falling stars,
past all the darkness and pain,
past the endlessness of our days and our nights,
and into something even god couldn't dream of…

Something that will be ours,
and ours alone…

WORDLESS

There is no poem delicate enough to describe your beauty,
no tenderness too small that it cannot be found in you,
there is nothing in all the known universe
that smiles they way you do…
How you posses my every affection,
how you inhabit the invisible strings of my soul…
Even your tiniest imperfections
are greater than all the untold beauties circling the Earth…
I love the way my heart pounds when you are near,
the way my senses are reborn…
how fascinated I become,
how I rediscover myself in you
and the sway of your hips.
As you breath in, so do I…
lingering on every rising inch of your skin,
with as much diligence as I would a shrine to my ancestors.
Those lips, what magic created them?
Where did the gods go to find such glowing jewels?
And how did they ever manage part with them?
I could not…
not for all the treasures available to mankind,
I could never belong to anyone but you.
You are wordless…

PILLOW FIGHT

I remember the first time I smelled your skin,
it was like fear and excitement mixed together…
it reminded me of what it means to be young and reckless,
it reminded me of being in love.
I was a man lost within my masculinity,
forgetting that there could be something as sweet and soft as you.
You lips were tiny pink pillows,
an when we kissed it was like a pillow fight…
the kind you have when you feel completely comfortable
and belonging with another human soul.
In our childhood we forgot how much we needed each other,
and in this moment of all alone and right now…
you are reminding me of just how much I want and need
to be loved with abandon.
I wish I could take back all the unkind moments that have passed between us,
like fallen flower petals being put back together…
but having survived the worst,
I hope that it will be the pain that teaches us to forgive.
The older I get, the less I can be sure of…
so much of the world is full of lies
but after all the doubting is done,
one thing remains true…
and that is your skin in communion with mine…
like a holy scripture of the soul
that all the world can read.
One day, all that I am may disappear,
but if it does, I take comfort in the hope
that some part of who I am,
will always remain alive in you.

You are the end of all my sentences…
and the beginning of all my dreams.

SIGNIFICANCE

God said, "let there be light…"
and then there was you,
shining in a moment of brilliance and passion.
And ever since that glowing Glorious gift
you have out-shone the stars in all their radiance.
Sometimes, but especially when you smile;
I can see the meaning of the universe
caught madly in you eyes.
If I have ever truly known the feeling of significance,
it has occurred from being near you,
and that pouting skin of yours.
Someone once told me that dreams never come true,
but he mustn't have known the curve of your inner thigh,
where hides all my boyhood sleepishness.
I haven't even a penny to give in exchange for your kisses
though they are of immeasurable value…
all I have are my words and my poor poet-soul,
and this I give willingly as an offering to you.
In exchange, I ask only for your sweet hand
to guide me into the here-after.
Press my head against your breasts when I am weak
and let me know home at last.
Love me now,
and I will be yours
in the infinity that is to come.

A CROSS CALLED LOVE

You half complete me,
and in our conversational lullaby there is poetry,
as we convince one another,
among echoes of our past,
that there will always be a tomorrow for us,
when we know,
all that remains of us is literary togetherness,
words of poetry,
written in hopes of predicting what might be,
but never will.
Our names grow on each other's souls like old thorns,
that we know need to be cut off, but won't...
because have taken root in the heart.
You crucify me...
on a daily basis,
nailing me to a cross-called-love,
whose nails go deeper than flesh and bone,
and whose shape defines our progression,
from lovers...to strangers...to love...
you are the stripes upon my back...
I bleed-for-you...
you wound me in ways that won't heal...
and forever is a long time to mourn for someone,
whose love hurts like knives.
You are the metaphor of lost love,
and in your eyes
are all my tragedies manifest.

A MIDNIGHT PRELUDE

Full moon yawning at me
from undisturbed night's sky,
howl of wind at my ears,
sent of you on air.
I climb the Weeping Willow tree which grows wild
outside your second story window,
manage meticulous fragile limbs
which lead to balcony's edge,
inch by wooden inch
cutting hand in silent struggle
to maintain balance.
Then quiet, feral…
take my place on
balcony banister
and watch you painting canvas.
Like panther in waiting,
hungry for you…
desirous of you,
diamond blue eyes
keening at you from
moonlit secrecy.
Tonight we'll make love like animals
with growls, and moans, and private purrs,
and I'll remember this bestial moment
of stealth in trees…
as a midnight prelude
to our love making.

A MOONLIGHT CARRIAGE

I see us in Italy
kissing in Roman cathedrals
the Coliseum, holding hands
as we walk along forgotten sidewalks,
of Picasso's palace.
Then perhaps a rendezvous to French quarters
of the Bourbon Street blues
like old New Orleans…
We, making love under a Paris moon
like lovers in love with being lost,
lost with being in love…
There is an ancient marina
off the coast of Spain,
it leans in the daylight
like a purpose waiting to be found,
we will be its completion,
as we set foot on distant shores
of that Atlantiean sea…
and finally to Greece
where soldiers fought and died
over the beauty of a woman
much as I would bleed for the honor of you,
and there, amidst a gossamer lagoon,
we'll dive into each other's souls
without life preservers,
and drown in the inevitable
tide of our love,
until at last
we can come home
on wings of starry promise

in a moonlight carriage…
and then,
let me show you America
let me show you our home.

ABOUT YOU

Tonight's sky reminds me of you…
as it softly kisses the moon,
someone is wearing your perfume…
it smells like sex and honey bloom.
The stars are undulating on satin sea…
as far as the eye can see
and it seems to be
a poem about you
waiting for me.

A ROPE, BLINDFOLD, AND LOTS OF KISSES...

I show up at door with fist full of flowers,
(hidden behind back for dramatic effect)
and box of chocolate covered strawberries...
you smile, we kiss,
and hold one another in a tender moment of hello,
then we're off to a romantic encounter with destiny,
which entails a dark candlelit bed room,
a rope, blind fold, and lots of kisses...
I make love to your belly button with my tongue,
you moan, breathe heavy, bite bottom lip,
and pull me on top.
Then begins our poetry,
words captured in candlelight of mad-passion...
where all I know are your lips,
...and all I can write is what I know,
which is you,
a goddess on my bed,
legs spread,
like a map to heaven.

A VIRGIN ON THE VERGE

I have come that the Sun might know the beauty of the Moon,
that you might know the meaning of night,
and that we might all look to the sky for our inheritance,
which is universal deliverance from tedious mortality
and mad mundane meanderings…
I have come by mutual consent of God and others,
to share with all…
the bright blessings of day,
and devious deliverance of dark.
There is more true heartfelt religion
in a single kiss of enthusiastic love,
than in all the spiritual institutions ever known to man…
more meaning in the laughter of an innocent god-child,
than can be summed up
by the whole of human existence.
Let me show you truth,
she is a virgin on the verge
of losing her virginity,
wide eyed wonder,
waiting to be known.
Kiss her just right,
and she will tell you all.

A WHISPER OF GOODBYE

In my mind we kiss an imaginary kiss…
with feeling less imagined than felt,
lingering touch
of suspended animation,
like dandelion on wind…
blown with the slightest of ease,
in slow motion.
In my heart we are interconnected,
by transcendental threads of destiny
being woven into a tapestry of forever oblivion…
called heaven, taste like honey.
This symbiotic nothingness
is the better part of my hopeful conscious passion to know you.
Tragic though…that heart and mind
don't really matter in this scenario,
because despite the best intentions of both
in reality, we are missing our God-intended purpose,
which is us together…
writing ourselves on a starry night canvas.
Instead we will slip quietly
through each-other's fingers
like only dreams can,
in a whisper of goodbye…
and years and years hence,
we will be only a remembrance
spoken by our forgetful tongues,
as they pass a time
trying to conceive of why we wasted our yesterdays
on such petty things as these fears we now own.
But as we part…

you to your life and I to mine,
please take this poem with you,
and in it, read my sincere desire
to be the co-author of our togetherness,
a book meant to be written hand in hand…
that for now,
will have to be left unfinished.

AIN'T NO HARM IN DAYDREAMING

I was just sitting here
thinking bout you,
…my first love…
wondering what you're up to,
imagining what you might be doing this very second,
laughing, taking a bath, falling asleep,
maybe crying alone in the dark,
(though I hope not the latter)
…and wondering…
if you ever think of me
like I think of you…
at odd moments,
when it seems that there's too many thoughts to be had,
and not enough kisses to go round,
…though I'm just a poor country boy…
who wouldn't know a poetic moment if it bit me in the ass,
I thought I'd write it down just the same,
cause after all…
ain't no harm in day-dreaming.

ALWAYS REMEMBERING

I've never had much,
but being with you always made me feel I owned the world…
and in your smile there was treasure enough for me.
This book contains the history of you and I,
our laughs, our tears, and our sad goodbyes.
We went from playing in the hay,
to kissing on the beach,
to making love by candlelight,
and always loving,
always in love.
I don't know whether this will be our epitaph, or our monument,
I do know that when history speaks of us, it will be with passion,
it will be said that, "They loved and hated well…"
and on some lonesome night when we are apart,
I hope you will take this book out and remember…
I hope you will remember.
Remember the first movie we ever saw together,
remember the things you said about me in your journal of privacy,
remember long distance phone calls,
remember making love in the park,
remember fighting and screaming,
and remember making up…
always making up.
Remember when we were in love…mad-crazy-passionate-love.
Remember wrestling all the time,
remember making and eating dinner together,
remember cheeseburgers and scary movies,
remember never saying I give up,
never giving up.
Remember a Prom-night disaster, and you needing your space…

remember me leaving without saying goodbye.
Remember our first kiss in the air-port,
remember our last kiss on the moonlit beach,
remember thinking I was The One…
I *was* the one.
Remember crying on my shoulder about your mom and sister,
remember the poetry that I gave you,
remember what it was like to have me in your life,
natural, unforced, difficult, but together,
always together.
Remember me inside of you,
you on top of me,
holding each other in the stillness,
after you have remembered all this,
think about what it will be like without me…
and know that I am remembering too.
Always remembering.

ALL THE POETRY IN THE WORLD

I think you are most beautiful
when crying under moonlight…
shadows of the never-ending-now catch your tears,
and I stand swaying by the truth of you,
which is timeless.
You are the infinity of my sad-endless-yesterday,
the mournful look of you, teary-eyed as I hold your head.
This is where we first made love,
on this hill, under these stars…
in this madness which is passion.
And this is where we will say goodbye,
in this moment of nevermore's and lost I love you's.
Kissing you for the first and last time,
in this dream-of-us…
not wanting you to leave,
but leaving you anyway, so that you can know forever,
the loss-of-me.
The tender emptiness of a missed lover,
feel the ever deepening chasm of regret,
cry for the times we will never share,
believe me when I say,
there is no more you and I.
And as you kiss me for the last time,
realize, that there can be no more tomorrows for us,
only the sad-forlorn-wanderings of our souls.
The hoax of forever,
perpetuated by a liar-called-love,
who says that love is enough,
and it is…for a while,
until the newness of together-and-always fades

into the broken sobs of "have a good-life"
and all our intimacy becomes some random phone call...
of forgotten days gone by,
where you tell me that you miss me,
and I say, "I know. I miss you too."
And together we wonder...
what tore us so far apart?
All the poetry in the world couldn't save us,
so what else can I say?

ALL THE STARS COMBINED

She was a raven with blue eyes,
and she stole my heart…
as if it were a seed dropped from heaven.
…and now she flies the night sky
in search of less hostile prey,
I think of her
as often I see the moon
pass over the Pacific ocean.
We used to make love for hours
in the wilderness,
or on boardwalks under stars
and black skies
of the infinite California night.
How many kisses have I lost to her lips,
how many unbelievable stormy touches
did we pass among skin and music?
In complete and utter exhaustion
of satisfied appetites,
like poetry completed,
left only to be remembered.
Her heart held more promise
than all the stars combined,
and the light of it
was too much
for me to bear.

ALL YOUR DIVINITY

Its the dawning
of a new day,
and I see in the sun
all your divinity
in the form of sunbeams
stolen from the basement of time
they shine on me
like God,
as I swim
in remembrances
of you.

ALMOST SAID GOODBYE

We discuss our future
over chocolate bars
standing barefoot in my forlorn kitchen,
tile-floor cold on feet.
Yesterday we almost said goodbye,
and I became older over night.

ALONE HAS A NICE RING TO IT

I'm not sure why I still write about you and I…
I guess it gives me a sense of completion,
something you never could,
and I think it has something to do with never actually saying goodbye…
only, "See you around…"
a very inadequate way of letting go of someone you love.
Knowing you has definitely made me better…
better at dealing with loss…
better at ignoring the pain…
better at writing things down…
you've helped me to become (in part) the poet that I am…
focused on darkness, mistrusting of love,
unable to let down my guard…for even a second.
Afraid that when I do find someone to give myself to…
there won't be much left to give…
too many broken-pieces of a shattered-heart,
and no one to help me collect them all.
And I tell myself,
"I've been on my own my whole life…
why should now be any different…it feels good to be alone…"
but that's a bunch of nonsense, the remnants of a lie,
that I must perpetuate…to cope.
Being alone has never been easy, then again…neither was being in love,
I guess there's issues to deal with no matter who you belong to…
even if it's yourself.
Still…when compared to the remembrance of you,
alone has a nice ring to it…
and it gives me comfort to know, that I don't miss you…
half as much, as I miss your warm body,
because that makes you easily replaceable…

to bad memories can't be bought and sold…

if they could, then I'd pitch a huge sign on the lawn of my soul that would read:

"Memories! Cheap memories! Nothing real! All second hand…and fake!"

I'm sure that no one would come running to make a purchase…

but at least it would be honest,

something you never were capable of.

I know I must sound bitter-angry-mad…

and I am, partially…

but when it all comes down to it,

I think I'm more hurt-disappointed-sad than anything…

because I thought, forever was a promise we could keep to each other,

but our love was an agony that we could not bear…

and the strain of it,

has left us torn…

and alone.

ALONE WITH YOU

I tell you that I have changed,
and you say, "It takes more than a week to change."
Why can't you see that it only takes a second to find yourself again,
a moment of looking in the right direction?
We all lose our way,
we all struggle in the darkness,
searching a lifetime, for what we have always possessed,
the truth of ourselves.
I never felt so alone,
until I was alone with you…
staring at me with those forlorn eyes of yours,
sweating from the inter-dis-course of our love grip.
You were always misunderstanding my silence for contentment,
not sensing the displeasure of my soul.
I, smiling casually,
turning over to mourn…
in the dark lonely bed of our togetherness.
I want you to leave! I need you to leave! Please leave!
So that I can at least have the dream of us,
memories that will haunt me…
while I travel in the lonely-American-night,
thinking of you, alone.
But no longer alone with you.

THE AMERICAN LANDSCAPE

I have been cradled in the arms of America…
bathed in her goodness.
I have known her beauty,
and discovered her again and again.

I call her my own.
But she belongs to us both.

I have spent a lifetime traveling her veins…
exploring her womb,
I have swam in her blood,
and would give for her my own.

She is the promised land,
over flowing with dignity.

She sustains me.
And in her eyes I see a piece of myself,
barely understood and often abused,
but beautiful just the same.

And like myself,
she retains a magic all her own.

She is the giver of dreams
and muse to poets .
with her promised-adventure,
and endless-possibilities.

She is broad,
and contains multitudes.

I have seen the very heart of America
it is a reflection of God's.
And as traveled as she is,
I see in her a frontier as yet untouched.

She is my constant companion.
She inhabits me.

She is the America of my youth…
proud and spectacular still.
For in the sweet bosom of my America,
lives her freedom-stained-soul.

She knows my tears…and catches them as they fall,
into the soil of her grasp.

And as extensive as my education has been,
in all those books,
I have never read anything so poetic…
as the American landscape.

AN ABUSED OPOSSUM

"What are you
doing…" she asks.
"I'm hoping…" I say,
she smirks in the silence
I sense her disdain,
and together we stare blankly at the ceiling
of her dilapidated house that is falling apart by degrees.
There is a family of opossums
creaking around in the attic,
perhaps they've gathered for winter…
I imagine them celebrating Christmas
without all the ills of human indifference…
but they're probably just trying to survive
like everything else in this world.
We can hear their tiny animal feet
patter across the ceiling,
sometimes they startle us into laughter…
and sometimes into fear,
but now the babies must be hungry,
cause they're crying for something…
or maybe their mother beats them
in the darkness,
like mine did me…
All these thing I lay contemplating,
imagining in my mind that I am
capable of understanding…
until I remember that we're saying goodbye,
she and I, on a bed of sadness.
And I think,
that even if it meant being hurt,

I'd rather be an abused opossum
with a family to call my own,
than a lonely poet
lost without her.

AND THIS IS HOW IT ENDS…

I'm driving mad…wild, 110 miles per hour,
which seems quick enough,
but my mind is racing faster,
I've already been home a thousand times in my brain,
rehearsing what to say when I see you,
wondering how it's going to be,
when we say our final-farewells.
The minutes pass like hours, the hours cliché into years,
and the misery is never ending…
I drive this ceaseless sad road,
which was supposed to lead me home, back to the arms of my lover,
but instead…has turned out to be another finite tragedy,
in a long line of painful-regrettable-sadness,
which usually begins and ends with me standing alone,
no one to cling to but myself
and now I hear the voice of my old friend desperation,
whose song is as familiar as time, but rings fiendish in my heart.
When I finally arrive at Our door step,
which has once again become Your door step…
(since there is no more you and I, only solitary you)
all road-weary and emotion-full, you're not home, but at a friend's house,
so I call…and wait 15 years/minutes in cold California morning for you to come,
knowing that when you do, you'll see me writing this poem,
and perhaps think of all the poetry we've shared,
or some other unreadable thought,
and I am sitting on an old battered suitcase,
that I use to travel world with,
and thinking…we are a tragedy you and I,
utterly tragic in every way,
the artist and poet under one roof,

making sweet love in sea-cold-coast of a 2nd story apartment.
Angry cars pass the door-step before you actually show up,
and I look at you with dread,
wanting to prolong our wincing miserable good-bye,
which I have spent all night fearing...
but eventually you come,
with your friend in the car like I knew you would...
because (secretly) you're afraid to look in my eyes alone,
maybe you'll want me back.
And this is how it ends...
no more writing in the book-of-us,
because all's been said that could be said,
all's been done that could be done...
so we cry, and embrace tremendous...
and I kiss you before I go,
and then am gone.

AS WE INHABIT THE NIGHT

Posses my body
like you posses my soul…
give me kisses
and give me life…
Let my name become
the prayer from your lips,
spoken at dawn
in the name of midnight.
I will be your skin,
wear me like the universe wears time…
finger tip to finger tip,
laughter dripping from our eyes
in the form of radiant moons.
Be the deity of my desire,
let me worship you
under the promise of candlelight,
in the bosom of purpose,
as we inhabit the night.

ENOUGH FOR ME

This moon causes me to love you by degrees,
lunar destiny,
the night belongs to us,
we are astrology's children…
nocturnal lovers,
you are the stars,
I am the sky,
inhabit me then…
make your home
among my spaciousness,
and I will fill the void
of your infinity,
with solar-love
designed from laughter,
because in your smile
is universe enough for me.

AT A LOSS FOR WORDS

I've been searching
for the God-inspired words
to convey your divinity
in poetic form,
re-write your presence
on this poor poet's page.
…and now my dilemma…
how to verbalize
what is wordless
by using refined prosaic-creatures…
sky is not enough
to paint your smile,
moon cannot describe
the sadness of your goodbye,
and there is not enough syntax
in the whole summation of infinity
to convey the utter sense of promise
that accompanies your hello.
I am at a loss for words…
all I know
is that somehow,
you make me swoon.

AT THE FOOT OF MY BED

I remember you…how could I forget?
You were my smiling-lover, whose lips felt like eternity,
and whose skin held more promised-possibility than stars.
We traveled tremendous distance you and I,
stood at the brink of many sunsets,
held each other under endless moon-lit-nights,
but in the end, it was sad goodbye,
words unfit for our kind of love,
whose passion was as endless as forever (or so we thought).
And as this vast expanse of road unravels before me,
I am reminded of you, because the sun is slowly fading over the canyon,
and slivers of half-light, resembling your smile, are thrown on plateaus.
I am refreshed with thoughts of then and never-again…
when we kissed, all the time, for no reason at all,
or simply because of the way our lips felt together,
the way We felt…together.
When we made love to the sound of our own breathing…
my eyes held the universe for you,
and your touch was the most influential reason to live.
Before tears, and regret, the miseries that tore us apart,
broke our hearts into countless-shards-of-sadness.
I think…somehow, as we were picking up the pieces
of our shattered-life-together,
you may have gathered a portion of me…unaware,
because…there is definitely something missing,
something that I can't seem to find, or name…
without it…I'm not sure I make sense anymore.
You were the adhesive that held together my fragile-tentative-self
and without our cohesion, life doesn't seem as poetic.
I've grown accustomed to the easy give-and-take of us,

(though I took more than I gave)
and as many lovers as I have called mine,
you'd think I would be used to it by now…
to accepting-the-loss of their kisses,
in exchange for an empty bed…
they managed to reserve a portion of my soul,
in order to make theirs more complete,
(like I did to you)
but sometime after midnight, which is the better part of good-bye,
they'd lost an intangible part of their essence,
much to their surprise, left behind…
at the foot-of-my-bed…
a temple more divine than most,
because it holds honest-soul-full-communion.
And that is what I miss most of all,
being able to know you,
in the holiness of our poetry,
manifesting its wordless-self
with tender kisses of I love you and remember.

BACK TO POETRY AS USUAL

You weren't supposed to mean this much to me…
not now, not when all we ever wanted to do was "just be friends"
(whatever that means…)
and certainly not when we both have ties in other worlds,
ties which will forever prevent us from becoming
more than what we could be,
lovers in love…
making poetry out of kisses.
But passion is no respecter of good-intentions…
turning every potential touch into sexually charged energy,
so that even being near each-other,
becomes a challenge to resist our innate attraction.
And my God! Your lips…your skin, soft milky flesh,
which speaks to my tongue in tender language of taste-able lovemaking.
…and this hotel room has become the hallowed ground
of our first consummation,
sweet holy caresses in fading dim light of TV…
Room 304, king size bed, made for this moment,
of tangled bodies, trembling in pleasure,
sweet moans of 2am sex encounter.
And I think,
"…how many trivial aspects of life
had to converge for us to end up here, like this?"
In each other's arms, in nothing but our skins,
in the middle of a moment we'll never forget…
an experience which will forever define who-WE-are.
Then we eat early morning breakfast…tremendous,
and say our 4am good-bye,
because I'm leaving for the next five days on a poetry writing mission…
but will think thoughts of you and I,

for every mile traveled.
Seeing in my mind now,
the eager unbelieving look on your face
at the realization of my member,
on the verge of penetrating you for first time,
images of stained sheets, tender kisses,
deep drink-like embraces.
All of which I will come back to soon,
but not soon enough,
and now comes the fear, of what if…
what if when we reunite, things are different,
our "more than friends" friendship turned into
shameful love affair over night,
if we fade from each other's lives, as quickly as we emerged
gone back to living,
back to poetry as usual?
It's the damn road, and it separates us by degrees,
creating questions like doubt in my brain…
but sometimes there are no easy answers.
Nothing left to do now but travel,
write, and hope for the best…

BE MY MOON

I will love you eternally
and without measure…
as the night loves the moon,
and so becomes dark
that she might shine.
There is no sun for me,
only the glow of stars and you
to fill my sky.
Not even heaven has seen
a love like this,
that dies to itself,
that lives for its beloved…
that calls upon the universe
to bear witness to such
monumental togetherness.
I will love you eternally
and without measure…
as the night loves the moon
and so becomes dark
that she might shine.
Be my moon,
that I may be your night
and so become dark
that you might shine.

BEAUTY AND LAUGHTER

My lips have a serious desire
to become acquainted with your skin…
soft milky white tender flesh
that is begging to be kissed.
Have your ears ever heard a poem
that sounds like you?
Mine have, it's called midnight
and full moon of the never ending sky.
You resemble divinity in human form,
sure you weren't born form the womb of a star
and misplaced on Earth
to be a light for all mankind?
I think women like you are the reason men
act like beasts sometimes,
you drive us mad with beauty
and laughter.
You are the poem
of heaven's own heart…
I hear an angel in your voice,
see kindness in your eyes,
can you save my soul?
I think you can.

BEAUTY AT LAST

…you are a photograph…
porcelain figurine,
made with such divine composition,
that the hand of God
can be seen throughout…
such a rare painted smile,
renews my faith,
and now I know beauty at last.

BECAUSE OF YOU

…because of the way that red wine stains your white dress,
like blood from heaven,
divine saturation of love making blunder,
where we laughed till midnight,
then kissed under full-moon till all our kisses were gone.
…because of the way it feels to be in your arms,
warm…inviting,
comfortable in that 'home' sort of way,
that precludes forever.
…because of sleepless nights spent arguing over nothing,
anything…and everything in between,
but then making up,
always making up with language of tender I love you's.
…because of all the little things that make you who you are,
I am writing this,
holy saint of my poetic desire,
because of you…
I write.

BECAUSE WE CAN

It feels good to breathe,
as if every cell in my body has become sentient
and taken on a life of its own,
my skin is laughing,
as are we,
swimming in kisses
like holy fish of kindness.
Feels like we were made for this moment
to laugh and hide
under sheets that we imagine as tents
with nothing but poetry to share
and only grins to cover our nakedness.
"Tell me a secret…"
I say with complete abandon…
you search, as you do I say,
"My secret is that I worship you."
You smile, hold my cheeks and say
"Mine too."
Ahhhh divinity,
that we have come to this madness
…which is us alone…
in front of someone else's fire place
unashamed like children
in love with childhood,
in love with innocence
in love with sex
and the sound it makes
as we slap skin
on crazy California fold-outs
and palettes made on carpeted floors

for our fornication,
as we fuck and frolic
under full moons,
half moons, no moon,
any kind of moon!!!
so long as it occupies our night.
…and sometimes…
we make love
like gods making stars
with such divinity,
such insight…that truth is made
from our sweat,
it drips down our backs golden
and falls quietly onto soft sheets
that reflect candlelit dreams
of our uncommon togetherness.
Feels good to cum
as I deposit in you
all my future hopes,
all my tragic beginnings
my forlorn wanderings
having found rest in your womb,
which is like home to me,
where I have come to dwell,
within its folding temple I rise and fall,
by its warmth I am comforted,
it is a cradle of goodness.
We light incense,
and begin praying to each other's skin…
asking for forgiveness for all our sins,
finding mercy through touch
and now we are redeemed,

you by me,
and me by you...
our flesh is dancing
twisting into knots of togetherness
that fill the void of
before we met,
but never knew existed.
All that we feel...
can be summed up in laughter,
a single grin
given in tender compassion,
of I love you
and let's go to Italy,
not because we should,
but because we can...
because we believe in our tomorrow
that is being given life
by our today,
which is becoming the best time
of our yesterday.
This is where our journey begins,
in this moment of holy contour
of kissed lips
held hands
laughing faces
and poetry,
mountains of poems
to write us out.

OUR BED OF PAIN

I'm not sure how things ended up this way...
with you at the top of stairs, wrapped in a blanket, face full of tears,
and me at bottom, bags packed, ready to walk out the door.
All because of a kiss that never happened...
and the discrete preference of your hesitant soul.
I stop just short of the door as you say, "Please don't go...I love you."
In that instant, I realize that you never meant to hurt me,
or to lead me on the way you did...
but that unintentional invitation has led us to this place,
this miserable night of romantic-confusion and childhood-nightmares.
I remember asking you if we could hold each other before this night was over,
and listened with disappointment as you said,
"I don't think that would be a good idea..."
and like a sad-forlorn-lover I say, "Good-night then..." and kiss your cheek.
And laying on a foreign-bed-of-loneliness in some strangers house...
I hope against destiny, that you would want to be near me,
like I desire to be next to you.
Despite longing I manage to drift in semi-sleep, as if my soul has left my body,
only to be near you in the next room.
That is until I feel you slip carelessly into bed next to me...
startled, I ask, "Are you all right? What's wrong?"
I am relieved to hear you say,
"I couldn't sleep in that room...Does my presence here bother you?"
I say, "No of course not...good night Wonder-wall..."
I am pleased that you choose to be near me,
and for a moment I begin to think that destiny is fighting a losing battle...
Falling asleep with you only inches away from me...
just in my reach...and looking so divine...
I dream of possibilities, and wake to the sound of a screaming cat,
whose incessant cries from the roof-top have kept us restless

on this God-forsaken night.

I notice that you are closer than before,

and your exposed naval is inviting me to touch you,

so I do…with gentle courtesy…I lose myself in the softness of your skin…

you moan, breathe heavier, and pull a little closer.

All I can think is that I must be dreaming, and I want it to last,

but I know it cannot,

our faces touch, lips pass tenderly over one another,

and you pull me on top of you.

Our passion is about to bear the fruit of our first real kiss…

when you say, "This isn't good for our friendship…I'm sorry, I'm sorry…"

You motion to leave the room, but I hold on and ask you to stay.

With reluctance you do, but you keep saying you're sorry,

and I begin to feel inadequate,

unable to fill your void…take away your pain.

We continue to talk, when we should've kept silent,

and simply held each other in stillness…

It's funny how words meant to heal…tend to deepen the wound of demise.

And so our peculiar love gives way to confused-rejection…

and I leave our bed of pain,

cursing you and I under my breath,

but you came after me, asking me to stay, telling me how important I was to you,

so I stay…kiss your cheek…

and want nothing more than to take away your pain…

but there are no easy answers, some nightmares we cannot escape,

just have to do what it takes to survive…

and as we fall asleep in same bed as before,

only now, four feet apart, I know…

this is what you are trying to do…

your just trying to survive…

and so am I.

BEDOUIN DREAMS

Time to move again,
put my life in so many boxes,
like candy containers…
as though it could be bought and sold,
auctioned off to the highest bidder.
I am haunted by cardboard…
package wrapping, old newspapers, bubble plastic,
these are the slip covers
for my meandering madness.
Poetic nomad on the move,
madman prophet screaming to the world,
secrets which no one is ready to believe,
but are true none-the-less,
they lie in secluded slumber,
like gods waiting to be born
I come I travel, I write I travel, I leave I travel,
I travel, I travel, I travel, I transcend.
Transience is only one of many paths…
all leading to heaven,
divine consummation of Bedouin dreams,
because even heaven has roads
and streets to traverse,
lonely golden nights waiting to be slept…
and I'm only one step away from
complete and utter enlightenment,
which is the first and original journey
called poetry.

BEGINNING'S END

…and I just now called you on the telephone
as you sit in that big bright yellow home of yours…
as you and yours
watch a movie from couch and floors
as if doing chores
because as you talk to me
obviously you and he
have got to be
in arms reach…
and I think naw can't be
that you've finally
decided to hook back up
cause you sound stuck
oh fuck!
What luck,
that I'd call at such
an awful awful time
but I was just tryin'
to return your call
after all, its no small thing
to be in between two lovers
under covers
of old and new
I'll bet you
must've seen it coming,
as you heard that he was coming
down to San Diego
what a way to go…
and I know the whole
story of morning glory

from here it gets kind of gory,
cause I foresee
a fight at 2 in the morning
as he is mourning
the loss of you
as you two
fight tears
from secret fears
of being alone
and this poem
is all about goodbye,
and I'm not trying to pry
It's just that I know the taste of goodbye
and sad cries
that drop from eyes
as the ties that tie
are severed
forever.
Sounds clever
but forever is forever
that means never
never again,
because it has to end
hopefully you'll still be friends,
then again,
every new beginning
comes from some other
beginning's end.

BETWEEN HER LEGS

L.A. traffic, gridlock…
200 yards in front of me
someone hits their brake lights
and in rapid succession,
like a sea of red blinking dominoes
cars come to a slowing halt,
I curse angry at automobile gods,
whose untimely digression
has postponed my hasty endeavors…
because I drive like madman with purpose
knowing that…
between her legs
is Eden.

BOTTLES OF YOU

This day began with
remembrance of laughter,
bottles of you
that I will carry with me
on today's journey
like wine waiting to be poured.

BROKEN PROMISES

Picking up the pieces of my shattered self,
I, groping in darkness, over the memory of you,
am reminded of the way you looked at me when we made love.
All misty-eyed and fortune-full.
You held my head so that our eyes could meet
as I pushed myself deeper inside of you.
You said, "I love you, forever."
And I said, "I know, I know."
And looking at you in candlelight of mad love,
I felt instinctively that it could not last…
this ephemeral-promise of yours.
So I pushed deeper inside of you,
wanting to lose myself
in the crazy-warm-sensual-goodness of your womb.
Your fist clench hands-full-of-hair,
as you call out to God while screaming my name.
You say "Yes!" and I say, "yes…"
And my heart is crying out "No!"
No, for all the promises I know you will not keep.
You feed me lies-by-the-mouth-full, unsuspecting…
but I know you, I know your false sense of security,
and I know the taste of a broken promise as it kisses my lips.
I wish that forever meant eternity,
but when you say it, it means
"someday, when I'm not sure anymore…I will leave you like the rest."
I know your kind of forever…it is the song of almost-love,
I remember silent hours spent lost in each other's eye's,
without regard to time, soft kisses of I love you.
And just last night when I looked in your eyes and saw emptiness,
you said, "Are we just gonna' stare at each other or what?"

And I knew in that instant, I'd lost you, lost what was, what never was…
and so today, just to be sure I said, "I need you tonight."
And you said, "I need to have fun tonight, to be young again."
I could hear the snapping of truth
as you broke yet another promise.
The one where you said that you would always be there for me,
remember; the one about, dropping everything just to hold me.
Do me a favor, don't make any more promises you can't keep…
because its tearing me apart
pieces of my soul mourn for us.
So seventy poems and three hundred nights of making love later,
our moans of pleasure turn into sobs of grief,
and your claims of, "I'm sure your the one"
becomes inevitable, "I don't know anymore"
familiar sounds of goodbye and remember forever…
and as we choose our separate paths, your walk away confused,
and I am left empty handed,
but with a lifetime full of empty promises…
words that were never meant to last.

CALLED HEART

My love for you
is brighter than day,
darker than night
more expansive
than the universe…
and yet it fits
within this
tiny beating instrument
called heart.

CAPTURED BEST IN POETRY

…kissing you on star-less night,
because Polaris and her sisters
have gone into hiding behind clouds,
knowing only the wet tender moon-glow
of your lips on mine,
like comet scream-gliding across night's sky,
smooth, prolonged, cosmic,
signifying what it means to be true lovers…
which is truth and infinity coming together,
singing holy song of timelessness and forever,
heaven, manifest in our kiss,
made visible by darkness,
born of night,
rejuvenated by day,
but captured best in poetry.

CASUALTY OF LOVE

Screaming at you from across an empty room,
and perhaps from an even emptier soul,
eyes glaring…fist clenched…feral-bearing teeth…
my face contorts into dark reflection of my jaded soul,
and I realize what a monster I can be.
As my screams echo and fade into voiceless cries from a sore throat,
I watch the tears run down your cheeks.
They might as well be blood from your wrists,
because I have once again succeeded in hurting what I love,
making you bleed with regret for time spent with me.
I watch almost unconscious with madness,
as your soul is blown to bits by my words.
Hurting you…hurting me…hurting Us…
as I systematically chop away at every tie we have,
until you are left hanging by a thread.
Vowing to drive you as insane with sadness,
as you have driven me to rage and beyond.
I scream at your weakness…your reluctance…your kind heart…
I scream because you are everything that I am not.
Because your love is stronger than my hate,
and because you keep trying to ease my pain.
But all I know is my hurt,
and all I can share is what I know.
Those screams are my battle cries,
it is my soul saying:
I will not love without a fight! Leave me like the rest! Let me die…alone!
I am scream-bleeding from the wounds of my past.
And no matter how strong I appear to be…
the truth is, I'm afraid.
Afraid of losing you to misery,

and even more afraid of becoming,
just another casualty of love.

CELEBRATING EACH OTHER

Somewhere on the edge
of the Pacific ocean
two lovers are losing themselves
in the eye of the moon.
Fireworks in sky,
to signify a new year
and they are making sparks of their own
on lonely Earth
as their lips caress each other
with pyrotechnic affection.
With each explosion overhead
there are tiny implosions in his heart,
he can feel the blood hurdling hasty
through his veins
in a frantic effort to convey
romance to his brain.
She too is finding feeling in her limbs
like a tingling rush of emotion
it spans the length of her legs
assuring her of the future.
As far as they are concerned,
the world is composed of two,
the he in her,
and the her in him.
They are complete in their togetherness
and this is what it means
to be in love
a warm blanket of skin on skin
being worn ambiguously among
a wide lost sea,

while the world celebrates its-self
they are celebrating each other.

A Constellation Called Us

Touching you in dark American night…
while driving down an anonymous highway at eighty miles an hour,
our hands exchange gestures of love and lust,
as we ooh-and-aah in this eruption of sensations,
speed-caress, faster-touch, swerve-moan,
we kiss…
and I strain to watch the road.
Secretly, I want to let go of the steering wheel
end it all this way,
passionately under the stars…
holding you in one hand,
and the car in the other.
You kiss me with your palms,
and dance upon my soul with your fingers.
Pulling over, we run to consume each other in the woods,
like two lost gods of love…
consummating the union of our divinity,
creating a constellation called Us.
And under this moon I can see myself inside you,
head bent, back arched, eyes closed…
as you call my name.
Deeper-faster-harder,
until all of creation seems to join us…
in this midnight-dance of ours.
With songs of wind,
and kisses of moonlight.
And all time melts into our togetherness,
as our love goes super-nova…
in a flash of light and bliss-filled-magic,
our souls dissolve into one cosmic-explosion

of true love,
and we are forever etched in the night's sky,
as celestial lovers.

CUPID'S COMET

The universe whispers
its velvet secrets to me
by way of poor pontiff Pluto….
and I write with stardust
on perpetual paper
of the cosmic canvas
called Cupid's comet.
Jupiter is in love with Venus,
who is vexed with the face of Saturn…
but Mars is a mad poet
writing red poems to the planet he cannot have,
they all are singed by the Sun…
who sings brightly for the Moon.
But she won't have him
cause is secretly sexing
some distant star called Polaris.
They send living love poems
by way of comets and meteors.
Uranus is a lonely boy who
hates his name.
Neptune is a celestial fisherman
vying to catch falling stars,
while Mercury is sweating from the face of
burning father.
Mean while…
our own Earth
is the loneliest of all,
she cares only for her children,

we few living things
that inhabit her soil.

DESTINED FOR THE NIGHT

"Its smells like sex in here…"
you say, as we re-enter your car,
after a dinner of "learning to compromise."
Just an hour ago…
we made mad-love in the back seat of your Jeep,
among winding roads and passers-by of bay-drive.
Head-lights briefly illuminate your lips in the tangled sloping night,
in a way that makes me want you, want to be inside you,
to know the wetness of you on me.
Sensing in my soul that this night will become a poem in and of itself,
because you look so divine in your nakedness,
that I am apt to believe you a descendent of Aphrodite.
You are the goddess of my idolatry,
and I worship you in the temple-of-US,
where lip service no longer carries with it the stigma of facade,
but rather…connotes intimate-exchange of pressed skin.
You spread your legs,
inviting me into heaven's pink-gates,
where bliss is contained within fleshy-folds of pure warm fantastic-womanhood.
We kiss each other lavishly…
then comes the reluctant-goodbye,
finally, home to an empty bed,
and I think,
"…wish she were here…to lay beside me in this moment of longing…"
I pray in my heart that God will allow the Earth
to complete its cycle of at least one more day,
if just to kiss your neck,
look again in your eyes before I am gone,
so that I can know belonging at last.
I die with every sad-second we are apart,

and am re-born in the exhilaration of your laughter,
so much for not falling in love...
so much for being alone,
I can never live like that
when moments such as these consummate our togetherness.
When every touch of our hands contains universal truth,
and I know, just as certain as I know the stars are God's own creation,
I know...
we are destined for the night.

DIAMOND JEWEL OF HER SMILE

Her spine peaks through dress,
she moves in silence,
through crowd…weaving,
leaving a trail of broken hearts and awkward stares,
I too gaze with desire,
wanting to know the personality of her lips,
in my mind we have danced on shores of endless possibility,
already made mad sweet love,
spent nights in each other's arms,
though she has barely crossed half the length of dance floor.
I swim in her presence,
almost drowning…
till at last she is near me,
in the most magic moment of all,
looking just past my shoulder,
into forever midnight.
I motion to intercept,
but am caught unawares by the voice of a man-child,
whose arms open wide to receive the diamond jewel of her smile,
they kiss, and embrace tremendous…
I sigh in the darkness,
watch her from secret corner of room,
imagining in my heart that his hand upon her cheek were mine,
and that when she leaves here tonight,
I'd be the one to take her home,
to a tender bed of I love you,
and always.

DIVIDED PATRIOTISM

My heart and my cock are at war,
and at present...the southern region,
has more resource than the north.
Here is the original dilemma of man...
I am torn between
loving a woman I'm not attracted to,
and being attracted to a woman I do not love.
What am I to do with such divided patriotism?
My heart fights passionately with
kisses and conscience,
but the living libido has more lustful fury,
and so it is
that the ground of myself
is in constant flux.
Whose flag will prevail,
which creed will be sung as anthem
in the years to come?
Alas, there is no peace council
to settle such domestic disputes,
only the agent of age
to kill off the one,
while seeing cynic
become of the other.
We are doomed to decadence,
and there is no cure
for being men.

DREAMING IN BLACK AND WHITE

I am kissing the living night,
dark with a heart beat,
pitch with a pulse…
and this perfect black body
is absorbing all my light.
Laughter and kisses
for hours at a time,
until there is no time
only you and I,
dreaming in black and white.
We dance,
and there is twilight,
moon and sun
in complete agreement…
until at last,
we are left with only
this fading memory
called last night,
and the emerging hope
of tomorrow.

DRIVE ON

The smell of leather and road…
mixed with a surreal California coast-line,
that is undulating before our eyes…
you wrap your arms tightly around my waist as I kick it into second gear,
and we're off…
just you, me, and the open road,
miles of howling-highway and dark-unexpected's…
and the night is keening at us from its black center,
telling us to drive on…and we do…
like forlorn lovers of romantic get-away's
we pursue the setting of the sun.
Liberation…freedom of wind…like a sense of knowing eternity…
wordless sighs which indicate our bliss,
and stars that call to us from the expanse of a moon-less sky…
telling us that the secret to happiness is right here, right now,
in this moment of growling engine,
and cold hands…
of rustling leaves blown by the wind-shear of this asphaltic-panther.
Relentless…like a talisman of infinite-prosody…
which ululates of dementia and screams its defiance to the world,
like two ghost riders, we have no past…and no future,
only tonight…only each other…only forever…
which is an abstraction misunderstood by most,
because it can actually occur in a split second…
like the moment between breaths…
where anything can happen,
and usually does.
This is where we get lost, in the madness of Us…
among winding roads…Pacific starry nights…open eye kisses…
and at the end of a very long search,

which entailed looking for that solitary wanderer that most resembles our-self...
poetic artistic musical relics of timelessness
and concluded with this night,
where we left the house to rent a movie,
but ended up taking my motor-cycle, and each other...for a spin,
that we'll never forget.
Growl...
shift,
clutch;
accelerate:
drive on...
Drive
on.

DROWNING IN LOVE AGAIN

Laying here in the half-light of my bed-room,
looking in your eyes only to see a miniature reflection of myself,
and this seems so poetic to me,
as if signifying the metaphor of Us,
lost in one another's eyes, and on the verge of losing it all, to poetry…
the sun-light has dispersed through over-grown trees
that cover my second-story-window,
creating that cascade effect,
which only adds to the already sexually charged mood we're in…
we kiss…touch…moan…laugh…pull each other close…
and feel as if we were made to be this way,
lovers…making-love…in-love,
but that's what scares me, the "in-love" part…
because I've been in love before…or at least I thought I was,
and let me tell you, it wasn't at all like it should have been…
it was nothing like this, what we have…this unexpected-poetic-beauty,
it was more like a nightmare in which I was being pursued
by an aggressor-called-love…
whose teeth were bloody from a fresh kill,
and who's lips were wet for the taste of my soul.
With you it's different…
unrehearsed…quiet…tender…
there is this overwhelming sense of urgency, as if we're making up for lost time,
like two people who have been lost at sea their whole lives…
and are just now making it back to dry land, which represents anonymity,
only, just before we run ashore, and are finally safe forever…
on this land mass which is called being alone,
our world's collide.
Love is a liquid…which is bursting through our hull's,
and as desperately as we attempt to patch things up…

with dry aloneness in our sights…
our hearts begin to spring leaks within their once impervious shells…
and we are drowning-in-love-again.
I've lived a thousand lives, with lovers that have shared my body,
but never my soul,
been so many different people with them, and now looking back…
I can see that they were only gravel in a road that lead directly to you,
and this foreign place…which is your bed, feels strangely like home…
and I wonder, if I stay with you, who will I become?
Or better yet, who won't I become?
And am I willing to sacrifice the possibility of future lovers…future-selves,
for a chance at true love,
which only causes that guttural-uncertainty and sense of longing,
for the press of our lips-souls-hearts-minds-art…
…I give destiny a gesture of defiance, and tell fate that
she can't have this love affair…
I'll not allow the loss of a treasure as priceless as you,
not this time, not when my soul has finally found a place to rest…
as a reflection in your eyes,
through the words of our poetry,
among this artistic-watery-abyss,
which is Us…
which is Us…
which…is…Us…

IN WINE THERE IS TRUTH

In wine there is truth,
or so they say,
and this just may be the way
to heaven, then again
we began this time just fine,
with a bottle of red wine,
parked on an incline
just you and I,
not far from my
safe haven,
inhabited by ravens
sex laden, with a maiden
which is you,
we two in this too tender
of a night, no fights,
just moonlight
you being held tight
and right beside us is the wine,
ancient friend of time
friend of yours and mine
which goes down throat like rhyme
feels warm inside,
as I find my way inside
your soft little womb
and this could be my tomb,
cause I just wanna' die
when we fly
like butterflies
chasing fireflies
in night's sky

feels so right
to be right where we are
under god-glowing stars
never too far
from each other's touch
and this is such a rush
a hush comes over me,
as I watch you play with divinity
you dance and scream
out your god-given dreams
that seems to be
somewhere between
earth and heaven
11:11
time to make a wish,
and I wish
that we will always exist
together like this,
that is my wish
what is your wish?
Pish posh
as we wish wash
in a play of skin
then again
we call it flesh
cause it seems to mesh
as we sex and flex and dress
our selves in each other's breath,
you know the rest,
is turn and toss
across our life long loss...
as we drive off,

hhhhmmmmm
in wine there is truth
and my truth is you.

ENOUGH SAID

Two days and no word…
tow days and haven't heard
neither voice nor sound,
you haven't come 'round
and now there's no message waiting to be found
even the sky seems alone
as I pick up the phone,
but sssiiiggghhh,
you're not home,
so I leave silly song
thinking perhaps I was wrong
about calling, and falling,
and falling and falling
for someone like you…
too good to be true.
Isn't that the saying that everyone says
when they're saying something that can't be said,
it all goes to our heads…
this love affair
that we live like prayer
occasional and light,
best spoken at night,
in secret beds
under bed spread
with legs spread
where we dare to tread,
enough said?

ETERNALLY

I begin a poem for you on my hand
it moves to paper like sand and
I begin to wonder how or when
this whole thing began…
and if or when
it will ever end
but then again,
I am reminded of when
we first made plans
to got to the mountains
to play in the fountain of midnight
under God's own light
of night called sky
just you and I
as we ride
and glide
beside the ebb and tide
of the first night
of our new life together,
who knows whether
it will be forever,
but it'd be my pleasure
to measure our time together
in terms of forever,
never will I
think this is wrong,
I felt our love all along
this long and winding road
before we knew I've known
that this would be our own

chance to build a home
in the throne of each other's hearts
in this fate filled start,
of ours
though often far apart
we've never parted ways
or wasted a single days
worth of kisses
or wishes
because this is
the ultimate romance
of fate and chance
of dance and glance
of being in a trance
called falling in love
in love with hugs
my dove
know this
ain't no justice
just us...
the two of us
in each other we trust
because we must
and thus...
we bust free
eternally,
you and me...
eternally.

EVEN ALWAYS

I love you more than the stars
love their place in the sky,
and therefore fix themselves to the heavens
like glowing god-jewels
decorating the night.
More than the Sun loves the Earth,
and so shines bright that she might breathe
life from her clay heart.
I love you without knowing why,
or how, or whereby it comes from...
I have loved you before there was such a thing as love,
only particles of kindness floating about.
I love you as the flowers love the bees,
and so send pollen kisses their way
that the world may know the meaning of honey.
I love you like a madman seeking truth,
in vain, in spite of myself, with complete abandon...
I will love you for as long as time exists
and then I will love you still,
even in darkness,
even in death,
even always
I love you.

EVEN IN THE GOODBYE

We drink bubble tea in the sweet dreams cafe…
where we first hold hands
and try to forget that we are related…
stars by blood,
but lovers by fate,
destined for this moment of tenderness
and what will your family say if they find out.
Dizzy caress of palms kissing,
I reveal the key to unlock the chains of tradition
its called poetry, I use it to give us one moment of freedom
it resembles you and it sounds like jasmine on wind.
We agree to meet later for a secret rendezvous of who knows what…
but for now, back to your house for a dinner of pretending
like nothings changed…
I am surrounded by smiling faces
of your forgotten family,
and all I can think of is you,
the casual way your hair falls on your neck…
demurely speaking divinity to me from across busy dinner table,
the angelic purity that I felt in your smile
the utter sense of completion I find in your company.
Your mom to my right,
your sister to the left,
and you straight ahead
like a beacon to heaven
shining as bright at the sky.
Laughter all night long…
until we make an excuse to leave the house together…
sneaking away to our secrets of each other,
and stopping finally at an old gothic cathedral…

middle of winter, snow falling, cedars smiling
Christians inside the warm obelisk…
as we silently slip in the back door unannounced,
find dark passage way to sanctuary,
and there…on wooden pews,
hewn from hallowed trees
we hold each other in holy silence.
Blue green light is shinning through the stained glass,
making us glow like water
as I smell your skin for the first time…
it reminds me of honeysuckle on summer breeze.
Then we pray to each other in the form of a kiss,
which falls softly on my lips
like quiet music in the Arabian night,
the smack of our lips echoing in the Vesuvian halls…
we giggle amongst skin and kisses,
then crouch down low on floor
so as not to be seen by the janitor
or some other Christian intruder…
An hour of magic-madness
in sight of God's altar,
my first and only kiss in a church
the first and only kiss that has ever truly mattered…
and then at the height of my elation
a sudden jolt of reality…
you tell me that it could never work out between us,
looking for some sign that I understand, so
I agree, but inside I am wondering at the universal sarcasm of our situation,
wrong religion, wrong relation, wrong reasons
for us not to be together…
in my heart I have loved you
before I felt your breath in mine,

but common origins,
and uncommon beliefs
will not allow us to coexist…
how trite.
Tragically we leave the house of God…
drive to a secluded dark snow driven clearing,
and jump in the back seat of your car…
where we pray some more
in the form of tiny fairy kisses on cheek and lip,
until all we can do is hold one another
in the warmth of right now and all alone,
knowing that this is something we'll never forget,
this stolen moment of possibility
will be replaying itself in the movie of our minds for some time.
Before we leave, we decide to dance in the freezing cold Canadian road
to a song chosen by chance and fate, ironic Marley like lyrics…
"I don't care what your mama say, I'm in love wit you…"
it is accompanied by snowflakes from the basement of time
as we spin in the night of our togetherness
with all our cares waiting for us at home…
This will be my first and last dance with you,
and all I can do is forgive you for not being free,
forgive you for not letting go of your responsibilities,
forgive you for not being able to love me like I love you.
In my mind we will always be here,
in the prophetic Canadian night
dancing on almost forgotten streets
in the middle of nowhere,
to the tune of creation.
I will be loving you from the darkness
of an American bedroom,
as you drift along in search of what's next,

I will be loving you in complete silence and secrecy
as I write you memory letters
and poetry from my Hollywood bungalow…
I will be loving you always,
even in the stillness,
even in the brokenness,
even in the goodbye…
I will be loving you.

FATE

Crickets are the poetry of night...
that's right,
their lullaby is a serenade to the moon,
yesterday they sang to us
under pale blue glow of neon runes
called stars, shining like life
in cold California sky.
Cerulean tears fall from heaven
as we count to 7
signifying the prophecy of this night,
meteors scream across our line of sight,
burning up atmosphere as they go by
lighting the night with passion as they pass
reminding us of our divinity
which is dripping from our skin
in destined droplets of human on wind.
Falling stars dance across the nights sky...
kissing our eyes with stellar stares
what a pair...
as our hands do a dance of their own,
called flesh and bone,
memorizing the touch of skin
which feels more like poetry
and less like sin...
now it begins,
we bring along big bottle of wine
to help us find
our ability to shine.
Now naked under God's own eye...
as we try to spy satellites in sky,

you point to a star and say,
"Let's name it fate…"
that's great, and then we thank fate
for this ride
and ask her to be guide
to your sweet baby niece
who's love for you is like peace.
Wild screaming like Cherokees…
lelelelelelelelelelele!
from beside the street
of mountain side dreams,
as the trees keen at us with leaves,
which whisper raspy on wind
like ancient friends
bearing witness to our decadence
in this transcendental nothingness,
as we kiss, and bliss, and bliss
and bliss and kiss, and bliss.
We spill big bottle of wine…
and laugh like children lost in time
of this endless rhyming night,
which will soon become day,
as we pray
that this love never fade away
but can't stay here,
for fear that sun might reveal
all our hidden insecurities,
to which we've locked and thrown away keys.
I call you love…
Russian dove,
as you smile with my name on lips
as I slip my lips in between your hips

and worship Jade thighs
with moans and sighs
of our fate filled high
which will soon die
only to be reborn at noon.
a little to soon
for you to croon.
As we lay like lovers…
loveless, but undressed
none the less
as you press
you blooming breast
against my stone chest
and we rest….
and the rest is poetry
or as they say
to be continued another day
or night, which ever is right
or we just might
fade away,
like dimming stars at play
unable to articulate
our unexpected dance
with fate.

FOR ALL TIME

I have scars that remind me of you and I
our brief time together
represented by something
so permanent,
so lasting,
so deep.
This is no metaphor,
its the constant painful reminder
of who we were
etched into my skin
tattooed on my face
for all time.
You were the rock
that I broke myself against,
and now…
things will never
be the same…
and neither will we.
So I touch my scars in darkness
a hidden effort to remember us,
in the silence
there is a knowing
and so I touch them
without knowing why
but I touch them…
trying.

FOR THE GODS TO READ

I have constructed for you
a tower of diamond in my heart,
impervious to loss,
so then…dwell in me,
make your home here,
beneath my lungs and ribcage,
in this fleshy beating mass called heart,
write you name upon its walls,
siphon your needs from my lips,
let me reside between your legs forever…
and you will live eternally in poetry,
your name, written in heaven's unchangeable sky,
for the gods to read.

FOR YEARS TO COME

Tonight we made a toast to nothingness,
then danced under starlit sky,
on open ocean moon break,
like mermaids do.
Then back to my place
where all our tragedies come true,
kissing me,
kissing you.
…what ache we give ourselves…
what utter hopelessness,
to be lovers
at a moment such as this…
while all the world is sleeping-dreaming,
we are kissing in dark lonely bedroom
of the American night.
At times like these…
I feel so close to you,
that your lips kissing me
are my own,
that your pounding heart
beats in unison with mine.
The silly paradox of our togetherness,
is that just yesterday I thought,
"to be with you is one of the loneliest things in the world."
But I know that sometime
in the years to come…
all our tonight's,
our forever never kisses,
saying goodbye
and coming back together,

will be the last night
I can never forget.
...because some part of me,
will never escape your touch...
you've been magically-sadly written,
in the poem of me,
and I know for certain...
I will be kissing you
for years to come.

FREEDOM FROM MYSELF

I have grown to love you so much,
that to say goodbye now
would be like losing a sacred part of myself…
we're grafted.
There is no greater or worse thing
than to be in love,
the weight of it,
gravity on my soul…
the light of it,
freedom from myself.

GOD'S POEM TO THE SKY

Heaven is earth's love song to the moon,
sung by a trillion star children,
whose voices culminate on the brink of forever midnight…
you are my heaven,
I am your earth,
this is our song.
Angel is God's poem to the sky,
given flight by sun…
written with wings of laughter…
I am your god-of-poetry,
writing smiles with stardust,
your laughter fills me.
Space and time,
have never known such togetherness,
as this…
to dance under waterfalls,
kiss by candlelight,
make love to the sound of music…
and in so doing,
write the poem of Us.

HIDDEN IN THE LEAVES

Just yesterday, we went to mountains,
and there…among bending-trees and wild-flowers
we made love…
5000 feet above sea level,
with nothing in mind,
but the thought of consummation…
holy divine poetic love making.
Afterwards…like children,
we laughed and walked hand in hand back to camp,
roasted marshmallows, and read poetry to each other by firelight.
And today…
we found ourselves lost in the wilderness
despite signs which read,
"Do not hike off Trail"
managing once again to ignore the rules
(which never applied to us in the first place)
and end up a mile from where we should be,
all cut-up and worn-out from our down hill trek.
Even now, as we drive the winding road back home…
in a topless Jeep,
all wind-blown-and-fortune-full
I am writing this poem in my mind,
hoping to capture some of the natural essence of Us,
believing that if I can…
we will never have to say goodbye,
because all our yesterdays will be written for us to read,
and even if I lose you,
or you lose me,
we will never lose, the poetry of us…

the poetry of our mountain top experience,
hidden in the leaves.

How Divine is this Thing Called Skin

I wake up to a barrage of kisses and hands on cock…
your naked self
pressed against mine…
rocking steadily
in passion driven nudges
as you breathe in quick interrupted breaths of
"I…want…you…"
I ask, "Did you wake up horny?"
"No…" you say,
"…but when I saw you laying here I couldn't resist…"
I smile, as you peel away each layer of my pajamas,
until we are holding each other in the most naked moment of all,
that second of hands on private parts and lips on nipples…
as we reel and route one another
into moans which echo in our 2nd story bedroom….
you say, "I'm coming…. baby I'm coming…"
with such an urgency,
that it excites me to no end,
and I thrust myself deep into your warmth,
and think,
"How divine is this thing called skin…"

How Strange

You say nothing's changed,
how strange…
when I think of all the pain
and shame that made us stay the same.
I strain to maintain
some sense of coherence
our past lives hiss like interference
as we experience the inexperience
which is the better part of bliss
and it's as if
all things have come 'round
like a complete circle we've found
our place in each other's lives
no more awkward cries
no more sad goodbyes,
no more unnecessary lies
to hide the side
that couldn't abide.
Now we confide,
we slide, we ride this
new beginning express,
which I must confess
has far less stress
than all the rest
of our days combined,
this unopened wine
of mine, that's gotten sweet with time
and that's no line
its the sublime
truth, of me and you,

or should I say you and I
and while we're at it we might as well try
to go as high
as the sky will allow
cause I know somehow
that this moment of right now
is no golden cow,
its the "once was lost but now am found…"
that sounds so profound
when written down
or sung out loud,
like some kind of god-cloud
proud shroud, now unshrouded
unclouded, and no doubt compounded
into legendary status,
cause we have this
thang down on holy ground
pound for pound
as we pound on the doors of perception
some sort of spiritual interception
bringing the conception
of who we really are,
two shining stars
who've come to far to stop,
what a shock
from 1990 and Good gawd all mighty
to this untidy today
as we stray away
from whence we came
all rearranged
but still the same,
your right,

nothings changed…
how strange.

HUGGING THE VEIL OF TIME

…next to me is she…
"the one"
woman of my heart's desire,
whose smile is holy like heaven…
…next to her is he…
-child son-
born of another father,
who never gave a damn about fatherhood…
….next to him is lamp-light…
:turned off:
to hide our reconciled kisses,
from innocent eye of child…
…tonight we'll sleep as lost lovers should…
(his hand in hers)
her hand in mine
hugging the veil of time.

I am Incapable of Bullshit

I dreamed last night that we kissed...
but your breath didn't smell like cigarettes anymore,
and I think that you told me so
some where among the relics of my subconscious,
which have chosen to manifest themselves in nocturnal-vision-of-us...
and I came to the conclusion...that smoking or not,
you are still desirable to me,
because I refuse to base my entire opinion of you, on your bad habits
and believe me...I have judged others for far less,
but there is something about you...
that unnameable quality that makes you so...
poetic...yes, that's it...you remind me of poetry,
and because of this, I can't get you out of my head...
I know what your thinking...ok, so I don't know what you're thinking,
but I have an idea...all-right, I haven't a clue,
but let me assure you that this is not some petty attempt to seduce you,
in fact...I'm sure that I will never get past that smoking thing,
Contradictory? Not really...
because I think that we are lovers on another level,
a place where breath fresheners don't exist,
and really have no purpose anyway...
because the only kissing that goes on here,
is the union of two souls, as expressed in poetic-word-sex,
where we manually stimulate one another's metaphorical libidos
with the power of speech,
or rather, written-words-of-sweet-nothingness...
and as far as I can tell, we seem to know one another
by way of mutual consent, as opposed to the show me your soul method...
which can be very tedious when done in repetition.
I've said it before, but bear with me as I write it again,

you are spectacular…
and no amount of words on my part could make you more so,
believe me, no poet ever wrote anything without purpose…
but to achieve a desired effect…
and whether this writing will become an
obscure reference to the power of us,
I do not know, but in the mean time…
before anyone else reads it, and before I revise it,
or should I say, manipulate it so that it ends up saying something else,
which is not so self-revealing, and that I really didn't mean in the first place…
then accept it as a love-offering from me to you,
written after the tradition of true-lovers,
with slightly less fluff, and a whole lot more honesty…
because where you are concerned,
I am incapable of bull-shit…
and with that in mind, I guess what I am trying to say is:
Put down your cigarettes forever, and kiss me right now damn it!
Or run the risk of never knowing what it's like to taste my lips,
which are wet from poetry,
and parted for you.

I CRY FOR YOU IN MY DREAMS

…and the more I think about it,
the more I realize that our dissolution was as much,
if not more, my fault as it was yours,
(you remained beautiful through it all)
I have this fatal tendency to dissect everything down to the molecule
and nothing looks good in atomic form…not even love.
You were everything I ever wanted,
in a way that I could never quite verbalize…
(poor-poet-me)
and tonight, as the moon does its dance in the night's sky,
I can't help but think of you, of all our poetry,
of the way you moved me to passion with just a smile,
of our very first kiss in your tiny bed-for-one.
The way we used to stay awake all night long,
just dwelling in each other's hearts, eyes, lips…
till the sun came up, and you were off to work.
I miss everything about you, but especially…
the way you used to look at me when I was inside of you,
call me Lover in deep whispers,
when the whole world seemed to contain just the two of us,
and nothing else mattered but turning Art into love, making it work…
never wanting to lose the passion of first kiss…
I never did cry for the loss of you, never…till now,
till I realized how deep you inhabit me,
till I said it out loud to myself…alone, in a Georgia hotel room,
with you in California…1000 miles away, (in more ways than one).
Funny but…I miss the small of your back, that tiny part just above your hips,
where the skin dips inward…
where I would deposit all my future hopes for you and I,
something so insignificant, but late at night, while you were asleep,

I'd put my hand there and pray, strange I know, but I'd pray for you,
for our love, for the world to disappear and US to keep on living in this dream.
But the ultimate tragedy of dreaming...is that eventually, you wake up,
and wonder if what you remember was real, or imagined...
The thing that gets me the most,
is that after all that we've been through together,
all the love, all the pain, all the tears, all the never letting go...
the best I can hope for now,
is to maybe have coffee with you in some distant coffee shop,
look in your eyes from across a blank restaurant,
and remember that we used to love each other...
stare, knowing that you are once-in-a-life-time-irreplaceable
lost to my insensitivity, lost to living this miserable life of goodbyes,
lost mostly, to my lack of whatever it was that would have saved us.
Which I didn't posses, and could not conjure,
Now, every night...
I cry for the loss of you,
am torn from the loss of you...
bleed for the loss of you,
I cry for you, in my dreams.

IMAGINE

Imagine you and I together…
alone, with no one but ourselves,
holding each other in the silence,
knowing that no matter what
we will always be this way.
Imagine that we can hear each other's thoughts…
and in our minds, echoes a lost song,
each word, a melody of undying commitment…
and as our tears fall, our hearts bind
to form a sculpture of eternal beauty.
Imagine never having to let go,
never having to say goodbye,
never having to worry if I'm all right
because I'm right there with you…
protecting you from what ever seems to harm you.
Imagine now if you will,
for just a moment,
that you and I are more than just two friends…
that we have shared an intimacy that is beyond words,
that nothing can ever come between us.
Imagine in your heart that we are meant to be…
that destiny and time will form a union that cannot be broken,
a passion that cannot be quenched,
because in every moment that we have together
there is magic.
Imagine all these things
and the million or more possibilities that await us,
but when you are done
know this…

that I love you,
and you don't have to imagine anymore.

IN BETWEEN THE SCREAMS

Saying goodbye is never easy…
but it seems especially hard with you,
because I have deposited in your lips
all my future kisses, all my angry nights, all my loving thoughts
and even my sometimes unkind words…
in a sincere desire
to share the truest me,
with the truest you.
I have permanently etched your name
on the door of my heart,
so that all who dare approach
may know your presence,
and see the scars you leave behind.
Even when we're at odds,
some part of me
is still holding you in the silence…
in between the screams
there is sentience,
the knowing that everything
will be all right,
because our love is destined
to out last the stars
in night sky,
we are fixed…
and can no more say goodbye
than the day
can escape the sun.

IN HONOR OF FOREVER

I remember driving 12 hours
on 3 days of no sleep
just so we could be together for 2 moons…
through New Mexico dessert with no air conditioning
and less than 50 dollars in my pocket.
All I had left in the world was you,
and you were my Polaris,
northern light leading me to love…
the one indication that all was not lost.
Too young to have money,
and too poor to know any better…
we made a go of it,
first night spent in a sleazy $20 motel,
eating each other alive with abandon.
Then to sleep in dreamy arms of tomorrow morning
and no where to go but out.
You take me to an old Indian reservation,
and there among relics of the past,
we discuss our future…
uncertain of everything but our love,
we promise to never let go,
to never forget, to always remember.
Then we split a $5 cheeseburger,
sharing our bites like I love you's
giving butterfly kisses in between…
now bellies full, day almost done
we take an old quilt from the trunk of my car
and make our bed in the shady park,
among winos and ravens
both cawing for a hand out.

I hold you close in the sparse daylight,
we sleep warm together,
spooning the sun away…
and wake to the rising moon.
Now is time to say sad goodbye,
'cause there's a star
waiting for me on the boulevard in California,
or so I think.
We mourn the parting of our lips,
and kiss one last time
in honor of forever,
and I'm off into the full moon American night,
alone again, missing you.

IN THE LIPS OF LOVERS

The sparkle from your wedding ring is almost blinding,
and as the light refracts in my eyes,
I am reminded of last-nights-love-scenario,
where we took off all our clothes,
kissed each other with unholy-passion,
and spoke of what it means to be lovers,
gentle…unforced…noncommittal…
with whispers of tender-I-want-you's,
followed by long pauses of soul-searching,
when we try to decipher the code of our hearts,
by looking into each other's eyes with prolonged wanting.
The rain is coming down with purpose,
and as it pelts the roof of this strange-friendly-house,
we dance a sensual dance,
in a bed that belongs to someone else,
whose laughter we can hear, coming from just down the hall.
Pulling back your hair, you lick your lips and say,
"I love the way you feel inside me…"
and looking at your face, in the half-light of a dimmed lamp,
I reply with courteous smile, you smile back, and we dance some more,
with a choreography all our own,
whose steps can't be learned…
only felt…and expressed, in the lips of lovers.
You stay till morning,
waking me with tender kisses of: goodbye and I'll be back soon,
and as you turn to leave…
I notice that diamond, clutching your finger, like a demon,
as if to remind me that you belong to another,
whose hands are better at hitting than loving,
and whose lack of composure, and self respect,

causes him you drive you away with fists,
instead of drawing you closer with kisses,
his indecency has led you to-my-bed,
where all your fantasies will be fulfilled,
and you will know the pleasure of being held,
without time limits, beer-breath, ball-games,
or any other distractions,
only the silence of our togetherness,
which holds more promise, and magic, than all his lies ever could.
I am his worst night-mare, and your dream-come-true...
because I treat you like you deserve to be treated,
with love, and respect, in the tradition of all great lovers.
We worship at the temple-of-us,
with an incense made from romance,
and prayers offered by the pressing of our flesh,
communing in the commonality of our desire,
to simply know one another...
by sentience of touch, laughter, and an occasional kiss,
the true language of lovers.

THE WHISPERING GAME

When we kiss its like our lips are telling our souls a story
that only they can understand…
and our souls in turn
are telling our hearts that same secret,
in a way that only they can understand…
and our hearts are whispering to our minds,
which are talking to our bodies,
which are telling our emotions,
who finally reveal the secret to us for what it is…Love.
But the whole time it is being passed along,
the ways in which it is conveyed remain a mystery,
the language that speaks it is unknown,
like that game that people play
where one person whispers a sentence into someone's ear,
and they pass it along to the next person,
and they continue till everyone whispers the sentence to someone else,
but when the last person reveals what the message is,
it's always much different than what began…
and know one knows how it became what it did.
Of course some say that the secret actually begins in our eyes,
who speak only a single word to our entire being all at once…
and that word is desire.
Once desire is conveyed,
it then seeks its completion in the form of a touch,
or a smell, or a closeness of any kind…
Soon the idea of desire turns into yearning,
and then longing, and if we're very lucky,
all our hopes become realized in a kiss.
Which brings us back to our lips…
they are the instigators of this whole affair…

they spend their entire lives speaking our language,
or falling asleep on our faces,
when all they really want to do
is to be pressed up against another pair of lips
so they can begin speaking their own language…
so that they can start the whispering game with our souls,
so that we can finally
be in love…
Let's kiss
and listen for the words
happening within us.
Maybe if we kiss long enough
they will last…
and so will we.

INVITING

You're like a hot bath,
inviting,
once I get in
I just don't want to get out…

IT IS ENOUGH

Let's pretend that yesterday never happened,
that tomorrow never will be,
and that all we have is right now…today.
Let's not apologize for all the painful words,
but just hold each other,
and let our hands do the healing.
Let's never forget who we are,
remaining true to ourselves,
and know that it is enough…to simply be…and that is all.
Let's hold on to the dreams we share,
be big enough to accept our failures,
and never stop taking chances.
Let's know that no matter what…we will have each other…
and feel whole, and complete, and smile at that.
Let's give what we have right now, and not worry about,
what's next…how long…. or when it's over…
and simply love while we have the chance…without question.
Because the day is coming when I will be gone,
and all we will have left will be the memory of what was.
So let's pretend that yesterday never happened,
that tomorrow never will be,
and that all we have is today…right now…
and it is enough.

IT'LL BE LIKE BEFORE

…been a long time…
and now that you're back
not sure what to do,
'cept maybe laugh
for all the times we've cried,
and cry for all the times we never got to laugh.
…come a long way…
from 17 to 27,
and look where it's taken us,
to the ends of the world,
where we wandered alone…
only so we could come back to the arms of America
and to each other.
…you are the day inside of me…
and I am the night inside of you,
we are the offspring of Adam,
children of God's original poem,
written like color across sky.
…tomorrow you'll leave…
and I remain here,
richer from your presence,
but emptier for lack you leave behind,
but I'm sure that one day soon,
we'll meet again,
and when we do
it'll be like before…
only better, wiser, older,
less capable of seeing the stars,
but more likely to notice them.

KISSES

Kisses decorate my bed
like clocks haunt a mantel,
sentimentally…
keeping time for no one,
but ticking still
as a reminder of eternity…
like oil paintings occupy a wall
royally…
with complete abandon,
of passion and midnight…
like secrecy and whispers
of lost I love you's
and hopeful secrets
born from the womb of
not supposed to,
and so must…
like poems to the poet
careful creatures
of imagination
written without consent,
because there is no other way
to tell the world
what its missing,
kisses from mind
tender, delicate, demur
kisses.

LIFETIMES LEFT TO KISS

Unexpectedly you show up at my door,
with your finger on the peep-hole,
but instinctively I know it's you, and I smile…
that exhausting drive home at six-in-the-morning was worth it,
and my soul tells me that I've found-you-again,
because holding you I have the sense that we've done this before,
perhaps on some lost moonlit night we held hands by the Nile,
and when your father wasn't looking I stole a kiss.
Our hands dance to the cadence of tender I know you's,
as we lay sleepless in my dark candlelit bedroom…
and in the flickering light your soul suddenly makes sense,
you've been my Queen my Lover my Enemy my Goddess my Forbidden,
I have kissed you a thousand times, and will a thousand more,
because fate and chance have seen fit to bring us together,
sometimes by torchlight, and other-times by light of a candle.
Still…looking at you, half in remembrance and half in wonder,
I am reminded of a time not so long ago,
or possibly not to far in the future,
when we traveled each other's souls searching for our other-self,
realizing of course that time was against us
we vowed to look-past-forever…
and so we have been constantly losing and finding each other.
From where I stand today, with you in my arms, I am convinced…
tomorrow doesn't matter anymore,
we have lifetimes left to kiss.
I'm not sure how much time we have,
maybe this will be the at long last we've been waiting for,
but while you are here, holding my hands kissing my lips knowing-me,
we will relive the passion of our lost-millennial-love,
together under stars born a million years ago, on the day we first met.

And when its time to say goodbye,
I want you to know, that I will not rest in the next life…
until I've found you again…
until all our yesterday's become the last kiss goodnight,
and we are left holding each other,
in the ever lasting stillness of now and always.
Only tell me that you will do the same,
so that we won't have to lose each other again.

LIKE GODS BEING BORN

We drink bubble tea and act like cousins,
but are actually strangers…
And I think,
"I don't have to know you…to know that I love you…"
we share more than blood,
we share a connectedness that goes beyond relation,
because in the genetic make up of your skin
I find my ancient desires fulfilled
long before I imagined them.
A billion-billion years ago,
when the universe was still but cosmic dust,
we floated around the same spatial trails
perhaps our molecules rubbed against one another
in the mystic nebulous of new beginnings
and in that microscopic meeting of ours
there was sentience at last,
the conscious establishment of new life.
And now, galaxies later…
as we stand on the same ground of an insignificant planet
somewhere among the lost particles of the cosmos,
touching hands, touching lips, pressing skin…
I am reminded of that dream of before
where we floated in and out of one another's souls
like gods being born.
I have known you all my life,
and will forever more…
we will still be connected in the echoes of eternity
when there is nothing left but time,
nothing but cosmic dust,

nothing…but you and I
and a new beginning.

LIKE I AM

You are the poetry that I write,
when I am feeling a part of myself
that is more beautiful than I really am.
You are the words that I speak
when I am inspired and moved to passion.
You are the dreams that keep me going
in a night of sleeplessness,
the person I think of when I feel alone
and want to be comforted.
You are the person that I can cry to
when I am sad,
run to when I have no one
and no where else to run.
Because you hold me when I am weak,
you kiss me where it hurts
and you love me…
like I am.

LIKE WE BELONG

She always loved me when she was drunk.
We, making mad passionate tender love on a moonlit beach…
and kissing her,
I could taste sweet-alcohol,
as it evaporated from her tongue.
"Touch me…" she would say,
my fingers sliding down into her wet center of desire,
she moans, "Aaahhh!" and closes her eyes.
Then she grips me,
strokes my throbbing-love-muscle and says,
"I want you inside me."
Without a word I pull her on top of me…
she sits on my erect lap,
and together we relish in the pleasure of our simultaneous-release
legs spread, bodies shivering, tears falling.
Sometimes I think I was born just to be with her in this way,
in ecstasy, and on the brink of forever…
holding each other under moonlight and shooting stars.
It feels good, it feels right, it feels like we belong…
she, holding me, holding her, staying together.
Not because we love each other,
or because we can't live without each other,
though true…
but because we want each other and nothing else matters.
That's what I thought, that's what she told me,
and I believed her,
because I wanted to, and because I can't seem to remember
a time when I didn't love her in this way.
It seems as though we have been lovers before,
and will again…in some distant-imaginary way.

In my mind we will be dancing forever,
to a cadence of tender-I-love-you's-and-lost-good-nights…
burning like two falling stars,
leaving our mark in the night,
in a blaze of passion-and-fury…
holding each other till the end.

LIKE YOU

Your voice sounds like sex…
she says,
after our first attempts at love making,
though unsuccessful,
(because pain is too much for her to bear)
instead we lay naked on ebony sheets
of post new year's eve celebration,
which began on rainy tragic night,
and ended in shining rays of our almost coitus.
Now she turns to me,
nudgingly, secretive, inhaling my skin
and says,
mmm, I love your smell…
What's it smell like…I ask,
like you…she says,
like you.

LOST IN SKIN

Sometimes your skin
seems more familiar
to me than you do,
it speaks secrets in the dark…
secrets which you own
but have never heard
only suspected.
Late at night
as you sleep in the quiet
of our wine colored room,
I am drawn to your cheek,
it half smiles at me
from the veil of love stained sheets…
we pass a time in holy communion
just the cheek and I
laughing at the moon,
then I hear the whisper of your palm,
"hold me" she says…
so I take your hand in mine
and make it my own…
until at length
we have created skin tents,
hands full of love
inhabit the room like incense.
Sometimes…at the most unexpected moment
you jump in your sleep,
startling me into laughter…
reaching out for me
as if inviting me to dream with you,
and I do.

I pull you close
in that warm bed of divinity…
feel you settle into me
focus on your breathing,
and find you there…
among winding roads
of our sleeping flesh
and dreaming hearts.
We are tiny gods,
lost in skin.

MAYBE

At first I wanted you…
then I hated you,
now I love you.
Maybe one day
this will make sense…
maybe.

MI POEMA

Last night I met an angel…
Angel Johnson to be exact,
she moved like bird song,
through crowd, to my table,
and there, we exchanged kisses with a glance…
danced in one another's eyes,
till at length we spoke,
(verbal love making)
then came heaven,
rushing to my ears in form of her voice…it said,
"Hello poet…I'm the one who has come to save your soul
from its broken self, in my smile,
you will finally know what it means to be complete."
I grin, lick lips, thank God…
mentally kiss her good-night in my brain,
but in actuality I am saying let's meet tomorrow under waterfalls,
and we do, among mountain and winding road,
we dance silly-tragic-water dance in underwear,
smile tender smiles at one another from creek-bath,
where we wash away all our sorrows…
kiss tremendous, tell stories of mutual pain,
which brings us to hugs…then back home, to my bed,
where this poem has its birth,
and just today, right now, we made love,
in my candlelit bedroom,
we spoke of rivers running into forever,
we did so with out words, but in kisses…
kisses meant to heal the tearyness of our past,
but will also give birth to our future,
which begins now, as I write this poem…

from that same bed where we tickled each other's souls,

where we called each other by secret names, and hold naked selves tight.

Now, she is gone, back to bosom of God,

where all angels reside, her smile making him happier for the wear,

…and I am writing her eyes-lips-hands-all in this moment of never forget,

and always remember…

which will make for my most spectacular poem yet,

because every word has been written to resemble her,

my Angel, my heaven, my sanity…

mi poema.

MIDNIGHT SUN

Being with you is like parking in a 15 minute zone,
when I know I'll need at least an hour and a half
to do what I came to do…
which is worship you with kisses.
It's being on shore leave during a major war,
everyone is scrambling to the fight
and all I want to do is lay here lazy with you…
memorize your skin with my lips.
And now the whole world is falling apart,
except this hidden place that we inhabit,
among gaze and touch,
tender caress of we've just met
and how long will it last.
How long can the Sun hold the moon,
day occupy night,
before someone becomes suspicious
and calls us out?
This sweet indulgence of skin
is making me mad with desire,
more magic than memory,
as if I've finally arrived at a destination
I never knew I had…
and now know fully
the Nubian eye.
Dark flower blooming for me
by midnight sun,
which is moon,
which is you
which is us.

MIGHT AS WELL BE GODS

Meet me on Plutonian shores…
and let's dance under a Jupiter satellite,
because tonight the moon
is made of manna
and the sun
taste like lemonade,
so we might as well
be gods.

MISSING YOU

Missing you is like
trying to hold my breath
I can't do it for long
without feeling like
I'm going to die.

MORE ALONE

The quietest quiet
is the one
shared between
two people together,
but more alone
than ever.

MURDERED BY ASPHYXIATION

From the moment we said hello,
we started saying goodbye,
as unspoken ease of our togetherness
slipped into broken-screams of desperation.
I used to think that love was all we needed,
but now I know…
that love is not enough.
I am angry at the tragedy of it all,
I am angry,
not at you, but at Us.
For not being able to make it work,
for killing what we had,
with bullets of misery.
And as the excess baggage of our souls
became to heavy,
our love suffocated under the weight,
murdered by asphyxiation…
that will be the inscription on the tombstone-of-us.
My voice is gone from screaming,
and my ability to cope is lost to exhaustion…
a fatigue of the soul that cannot be remedied.
The whole universe seems to be dying from our loneliness.
And as the distance between you and I increases,
so do the tears of pain from your eyes.
With nothing in common, and even less to work with,
we made a go of it…
but your tenderness and my rage never made for good company.
This is what happens when friends become lovers,
and become enemies in the end,
this is the mess that is left to clean up after the fall.

I watch as the only person I have ever truly loved,
(with that sort of conscious love)
walks out my bedroom door for the last time...
and with tears in her eyes,
turns around to say goodbye.
I never thought it would end this way,
or maybe I always knew it had to,
but I stayed anyway,
because nothing can change the fact that I love you,
and even if I have lost you,
at least I defied fate, and won...
because no matter what happens,
we will always be together,
in my poetry.

MY HEART'S FIRST WIFE

It's never been easy saying good-bye to you,
but this time seemed...
especially difficult.
Lost in those God-hewn eyes of yours,
kissing gentle lamb lip
of our forever-never-togetherness.
And now dear angel,
I am reminded of our stolen past...
all the nights spent without you,
alone, in a bed made for two,
of kissing you goodnight,
and caressing your cheek in the mental morning of my mind,
where I imagined our consummation,
where I continue to fall in love with you,
on written poetic pages.
My heart's first wife...
I morn the loss of what we had,
what we may never have again,
destined divorce of a make believe marriage.
Still...you are,
and will forever be,
my first true love,
and therefore,
retain that portion of my heart,
which is most sacred...
rare, inaccessible,
yours.

MY TESTAMENT OF ALMOST LOVE

I would have ripped the stars from their cradle to be with you,
founds ways to defy the sun and moon,
by hiding sunshine and moon-glow in my pockets
only to give to you as token of my affection.
You cannot imagine how far I was willing to go
for the hint of a kiss,
what pains I took to contain my desire…
how utterly selfless I could have been
when it came to you.
There is no precedence for the intensity with which I felt,
to claw at my chest
in hopes of finding my soul for you,
to cry for you,
recreate the world for you,
find the heart of God for you…
for you,
all for you,
my testament of almost love.

NEVER MADE TO SHINE

We were walking along
busy streets of a cold
California night…
passing venders and merchants
hungry to make a deal…
Without a word
I bought you a star
for 20 dollars
because I wanted you to feel loved…
you smiled, took it home
and tried to hang it form your ceiling.
It broke into pieces,
like our love…
so much cardboard
glowing at first
but never made to shine

NEVER TO KISS AGAIN

I am writing these words,
though you will never read them,
(because have grown callous to my poetry)
so that the world will know forever, the loss of us.
Never since time of Eden,
has tragedy been felt so great,
nothing so utterly hopeless as our sad senseless goodbye.
Which we said in sentimental awkward way on ocean-front-pier,
with wind at our ears,
and tears in eyes,
we kissed, then went separate ways...
never to kiss again.
Stars have crumbled under less weight than we bore for one another,
moons-shattered, comets collided, whole universes collapsed,
with less force than we loved...
such monumental togetherness should be written,
for all to read,
though can be felt more readily in nights sky.
We are the ultimate human drama,
our love, lost to the expense of too much humanity...
but our tears captured forever here,
on this page of poetry,
which is actually a tombstone,
an epitathal inscription...
which signifies the death of hello,
and with it,
the birth of goodbye.

NOT ENOUGH

How many silly sad goodbyes did we say
before actually saying goodbye?
How many tears did we shed
over the thought to losing one another
before we finally lost one another?
How many lonesome nights did we spend apart and alone
before ultimately being apart and alone?
How many moments of madness
passed between our lips
before the passing made us mad?
How many questions did we have for one another
before the answers weren't enough?
How many second chances did we permit
to invade our better judgment out of desperate hope?
How many poems will I write
before I'm rid of you?
How many scenarios will we replay in our heads
saying, "if only" with tragic whispers?
How many times can we relive the past,
in order to forget the future?
Not enough,
as many as the stars in the sky,
but not enough.

One Last Dance

We dance to music that only we can hear,
silent cadence of the mind.
Moving to an imaginary melody,
we choreograph our steps through time.
Stride after stride,
we twist and we turn,
with each new moment a motion,
with each new movement we learn.
The song continues to change,
with each passing day.
The tune goes in or out,
the memories fade away.
Until at last, we are left standing still.
Our lives better for the wear,
our hearts charged from the thrill.
So we walk away and leave things unsaid,
unaware that tomorrow our lives may be read.
Like notes from a song,
we sound and can be heard,
and in our stanzas we leave behind words.
So let us arch our backs,
and let out a blast,
we must make it count,
or it may be our last.
Thus we find our way through the night,
and on musical wings we make our flight.
So before its all over take your chance,
don't be afraid to ask, for one last dance.

OUR PATH IS NIRVANA

Tell me about forever…
I say under soft glowing candlelight.
"Forever…is this moment, right now."
You reply with whispers in ear.
We laugh, and get lost in skin
among silhouettes of our timelessness
and giggles of almost forgotten secrets.
I kiss you with holy lips
that mythologize our love in
ritual teeming incantations
of the golden eternity.
We are the living Diamond Sutra,
our path is nirvana.

OUR SECRET POETRY

So where do I start?
With the first touch…that's when it began,
this crazy love affair of ours…
of secret rendezvous in public places,
acting like friends among our peers,
and privately kissing till dawn in the driveway…
you and your morals, me and my girlfriend, we both have promises to keep,
only yours are to yourself, while mine are to my present companion.
Neither of us are keeping our commitments very well,
as we lose our clothing piece by piece in a dark room
with your son just down the hall asleep on the couch,
he was running fever so we had to pick him up,
because nothing was about to keep us from exploring the softness of skin…
which we did in deep draughts of flesh on flesh
of moans in the silence of our tactile ballet,
where we feel the shape of one another with eyes wide open,
and see nothing but the soft glow of our togetherness in this
moment of lost beginnings and illicit affairs,
and as we lie spent on the sheets I think,
"Now this is something worth writing about…"
and know instinctively that I can't help but record this sin
which may lead to my down fall,
but everyone deserves to have secrets that they keep
from everyone but each other…
and this is ours, our secret poetry, our kiss of if only…
if only things were different,
if only we had more time,
if only we could resist the temptation of each other's lips,
then there would be no us, no last night, no remembrance of stolen time,
no record of the magic which took place in the arms of night,

only the sad forlorn sense that something is missing, something
which couldn't be pinpointed or given name,
something that without, would make us both less complete in our
incompleteness…
I treasure every heartfelt grip of your hands on mine,
the vulnerable way in which you looked at me with eager eyes,
as if offering me a portion of your soul in exchange for a piece of mine,
but neither of us have enough of ourselves to share, and even less time,
yet you insist on talking,
when all we should have done was follow our instincts of mad-love,
even as we slowly come to the conclusion that as far as we are concerned,
there really is no tomorrow,
I find myself regretting only one thing,
passing up the opportunity to shower with you,
in the madness of it all
I was inclined to spend more time touching you in the dryness of a water-bed,
but passion is not economic, and is no respecter of time limits,
we should have spent the night together caressing instead of obeying our fears,
perhaps next time, when we're both in the same place at the same time,
and we've nothing to hold us back from our desires,
we'll make love like love should be made,
in pure-poetic-passion, with no where else to be,
but in each other's arms.

POETRY IN FORM OF MUSIC

Met you for first time on a dance floor,
smiling to the sound of disco…
sweating from African groove,
you say hello…
I say hheelloo,
drawn out like western movie star,
in old B movie…
immediate connection in ether,
we gaze from poetic paradigm,
and recognize by osmosis,
that all things have come to this point,
suns and moons have aligned that we might be here,
in the same place at the same time…
dancing…
dancing because we know no other way,
than to worship heaven with sweat,
sacrificing feet to music…
visualizing tomorrows, kissing forever…
with truth,
which is poetry,
poetry in form of music.

THE POETRY THAT KEEPS US TOGETHER

Calling you again for first time, in long time…
reviving easy give and take of us,
you used to say, "I'm so glad I met you…you challenge me."
I wonder if you still feel this way,
because loyalty and trust were our oaths-of-the-past…
I say, "Let's have lunch together…" and you agree,
and watching you pull up in my drive-way,
I get the feeling that its going to be all-right,
we'll get back to where we were, and perhaps travel further.
I remember late nights spent deep in conversation,
laughing for no reason at all, knowing how real we could be,
then without a word I was gone…consumed by the darkness,
and you were left standing alone,
wondering what the hell happened.
As I emerge from self imposed cocoon of misery,
I can't help but look for you,
hungry for the companionship of your-smile,
its funny…you never ask where I've been,
somehow I think you understand…
I have been paying for my sins.
I listen as you read your poetry,
and am glad to be a-part-of it,
a-part-of the honesty, a-part-of what was,
knowing that each press-of-ink in that notebook of yours…
represents some part of who-we-were, and who-we've-become.
I know you, I know your voice and in a way your soul,
still, there are miles-of-togetherness left to travel,
secret thoughts of who-knows-what that will bring us home.
It's the poetry that keeps us together,
words-of-I'm-sorry-and-it's-ok, written to make us understand.

We have poems left to share, creating the text-of-our-truth,
which is never-ending-moments-of-now captured to be remembered…
and on some distant tomorrow,
we will open books that we've created, and read each other out loud,
we will remember one another as poems-of-the-past,
and we will still be writing,
writing our yesterday's onto paper of forever.

RANDOM ARGUMENT

There is a transparent-gray toothbrush
which now resides next to me
in the front seat of my car…
previously, it spent 6 months hovering
near your bathroom sink,
watching over our togetherness
like a bristly mouthed sentinel,
its presence there
was indication that we'd not let go,
its absence, a sad symptom of our demise.
On five separate occasions
it was hastily withdrawn from its resting place,
only to be returned the following day, along with hugs.
Today marks the seventh day of its most recent departure,
and the infinite sadness of our sudden goodbye.
Too many words, and not enough kisses…
this was the theme of last night's
lonesome coexistence, because
compromise is an animal
whose ways are hard to tame,
and ego is not a harness
for reaching reconciliation.
We all to often
practiced the art of throwing daggers,
word-knives
intended to pierce our hearts,
never saying I love you quite enough
to make it last.
And now,
I drive angry,

quiet, sad, alone…
wind reminding me of us,
toothbrush whispering your name,
speed odometer broken,
like silly poet heart mine…
all because of some
random argument.

RAVEN KISSES

Salty lipped kiss,
from jagged mountain peak,
walk weary we,
who've climbed its vertical length.
Nearer to sky,
circled by dark winged bird of poetic desire,
riding wind like promise…
we kiss raven kisses,
in honor of waterfalls
and forest trees,
crushed flowers
your lips speak to me…
despite our enemy,
which is time…
we need more time.

REDEEMED

More and more you listen to
less and less of what I say…
this is a symptom of something far worse
than simple neglect…
it is a byproduct of our loss
of what ever it is that makes things right
when people begin to drift apart
but find each other in the end.
I can't remember the last time we kissed
without having to fuck first,
and that is something I never wanted for us…
to be the couple that we promised we'd never become.
Where did we lose it?
How did we get this far without
noticing that our hearts were left behind?
I wish I could take back
all the angry words
passed between us,
and replace them with
tiny kisses on your cheek,
maybe then we'd still be in love,
maybe then we still understand
what it meant to feel something
other than bitterness for each other,
who knows, maybe
just maybe
we could be redeemed.

REFRESHED

I love taking naps with you in the day time…
chimes whisper tingly secrets to one another,
as the sun peers bashful through trees
that cover our second story
bed room window.
It reminds me of Greece in the summer time,
quiet and hidden…
to know that the outside world is busy
trying to get somewhere,
and here we are,
in no hurry to leave…
making silent sleepy love
to pillows with our cheeks.
Ceiling fan dancing like angel above,
the distant swish of passing cars,
a child laughs under our tree,
and dogs bark playful in mid afternoon.
We touch just kissingly,
barely moving under cotton down quilt…
until all motion comes to a weary being
in our slumber.
Then, we wake
to sound of birds
on balcony,
refreshed.

REMIND ME OF GOD

Its raining,
and all I can think is to hold you...
in this wet tender moment
of all alone and new beginnings,
where we dance to the tune of rolling thunder
and the sound of our synchronous breathing,
accompanied by howl of wind
and swish of swaying trees.
Your lips remind me of God.

RESCUED BY HOPE

Last night we dove deep
into each other's skin
as though we could swim forever
among wet liquid flesh…
our lips like warm water spilling
onto one anthers bodies…
and our eyes finding true north
as they linger together
in quiet moments of
tender love and
spent touch…
almost lost
to madness,
but rescued
by hope.

SALVATION IN THE FORM OF FLESH

The kind of woman men die for,
whole kingdoms have been fought and lost
over your kinship…and here am I,
like a secret creature,
sharing in the goodness of your womb.
I see you on the shores of Greece,
taken from Troy by the gods
to satiate a promise made to mortals.
…and now men are dying in tents
from wounds gained at battle
over the lips of you…
which I am quietly kissing
under dark moonlit night.
I steal touches from you,
and your skin
redeems my thievery.
Poor patriarch Achilles,
must face his own
half destined demise
while we are hiding tenderly
in the name of midnight,
under forgiving stars
that conceal our sins
with constellations.
My father Zeus
has sent me here
to explore your divinity,
which is dark deep folds
of warm womanhood…
and between your nocturnal thighs

I have found salvation
in the form of flesh.

SAYING GOODBYE

Old habits die hard,
and staring at phone…
I fight urge to call you.
As I turn on my TV
I turn off my heart…
and I wonder if that is all you have become to me,
just another habit.
If what we once called love,
has become an added convenience…
and if the joy of hearing your voice
has turned into an automated response,
then what's left for us to do, but say goodbye?
I love you,
I mean, I know I loved you…
but I'm just not sure anymore.
I can barely see through the haze of our discord,
and when I finally do get through,
there are still walls of insecurity left to climb.
You were my friend,
who became my lover,
and now you are just another fading memory.
At least that's what I tell myself.
This is the epitaph of our togetherness…
and as the last tear falls from my eyes,
I wipe away my past-life with you.
As I contemplate these things my phone rings…
you ask me how I'm doing.
I say "fine," you say, "That's good."
When I tell you its over,
you say, "I know, I've always known."

"Known what?" I ask.

"I've always known that you weren't capable of commitment" you say.

Then why did you stay with me I ask,

"Because, I love you…" you say.

"Because I love you."

And then you are gone,

and all I can do is cling to my regret like an old friend.

Because the fact is…

I love you too.

Goodbye…

SHEETS THAT YOU'VE JUST WASHED

I love to kiss your body in darkness…
tongue on nipple…hands on inner thigh…skin on skin…
ancient dance that is as old as time,
first performed by the stars and moon,
and handed down to us from the night's sky…
I know by heart the curves of you,
can sense the sounds of your urgency,
which translate into moans-and-whispers.
Candlelight, Indian-music, foldout couch,
in apartment not far from ocean,
and even closer to the airport,
how paradoxical this seems to me,
that we can at one moment,
be making love to the soft crashing of waves,
and in the next,
overwhelmed by jet engines…
screaming their turbine tune in the darkness of our consummation.
Stimulation erotica, sensory overload,
on verge of losing sanity to pleasure,
and becoming…and be-coming…and be cuming…
again and again, until all sense of our fatigue is forgotten,
and we lie together…spent, on sheets that you've just washed,
and which will need washing again soon.

SOMETHING BEYOND POETRY

Driving home in dark-pouring-rain,
I've traveled a hundred miles and have a hundred left to go,
listening as Jim Morrison sings, "This is the end…"
I motion to dry eyes and catch a sense of you,
the unfamiliar sent of your hands is caught on mine,
it's funny…but you smell like magic.
The press of your lips is still speaking to me,
and thoughts of you keep me awake on this fortune-less night,
smiling-out-loud…I swerve in my memory-of-you.
This has been our first and last chance-at-together,
and taking you home from a night of laughter,
I tell you…this is poetry we are poetry you are my poetry,
you smile and tell me that you are flattered by my words,
and holding your head I get the sense that you are uneasy,
flattered, but uneasy…
I asked you for one-good-night spent searching-emotional-bounds
and you gave me a dozen I-don't-understand's,
but you held my hands, and right now…that's all that matters.
Realizing of course that our-night is drawing to a close,
I say, "Dance with me in the rain…"
you smile and say, "Yes…" and I am satisfied.
As we approach our point of destination,
that threshold of never-again-and-always-remember,
I take your hand and ask, "May I have this dance?"
We take off shoes, the moment we touched it began to rain.
Bare-foot-and-freezing we dance…to the sound of water,
I pull you close, and talk-of-us,
you say, "Don't talk into my ears…they're sensitive…"
you tell me they are sensitive in that way that drives you crazy.
We wonder who invented dancing-and are glad that they did,

you tell me, "See, we're friends, friends can do this..."
I offer to show you what else friends can do, but your afraid,
and all I can think is how wonderful-this-moment-tastes.
Its 3am and we are dancing... a-wet-cold-tender-dance-of-maybe,
but not really...then leaving the rain I take you home,
before I go you read me your-poem-of-us...
written unintentionally, but honest just the same,
I cry, you are moved by my tears,
we hold each other in long-emotion-filled-moments,
and agree to not-try, agree to let-go, agree to one-kiss...
in that second-of-soft-union I live a lifetime with you,
something beyond poetry,
you gave me what I've been looking for...a glimpse-of-you.
All-weary-eyed with phone-in-hand you drift to bed,
and I pass your second-story-window with that image in mind,
yes...when something important is happening, silence is a lie,
that's what you told me, and then you were quiet,
as if to say, "I'm sorry, but you were mistaken, so let-it-go."
All right Love...I'll let-it-go, so you can be comfortable,
so that things can make sense again...at least for you.

STOLEN ROSES

So I stop by your second story apartment,
(hoping to illicit a kiss)
with another fist full of stolen roses…
which I managed to take from some unsuspecting suburban resident,
whose flower garden seemed to be 'too full' of perfect crimson-creatures,
so I thought I'd help em' get rid of a few…
or so I tell myself,
but the truth is, I like stealing roses,
(especially for you…)
makes the night seem more eventful if I can do something devious
in your honor, and get away with it…
also, tokens of affection gotten 'in-the-line of fire' as it were,
are ones worth remembering,
even after they're gone,
you can still hear the laughter of their misbegotten beginnings.
So all gardeners with green thumbs be-ware!
There is a rose thief about,
and he will steal your prize buds,
despite your best efforts to keep them safe,
he will do so in the name of romance,
under moonlight, for a woman…
so long as he can trade them for kisses.

SUGAR COATED SHEETS

She shows up at my door,
with a bottle of chocolate syrup,
and a can of whip cream,
wearing only a smile.
"Come in." I say,
and she does…
without hesitation
we are dancing on my bed,
to the tune of sex and sweets.
Red hair and green eyes
peek at me from sugar coated sheets,
sticky hands and licked lips kiss my body
to the brink of candy covered coitus.
Caramel covered breast,
juice induced thighs,
soft pallet of lower belly,
and she sighs
in candlelight
under a full moon…
then we're done,
and sleep warmly,
close in cold
California Night.

SWIMMING IN BEAUTY

When the day is done,
and darkness falls
and I'm alone with my thoughts...
I find company in the memory of you.
The moon's crescent reminds me
of your glowing smile,
the stars shine, but
only half as bright as your eyes
yet they have sufficed in
gathering together as much light
as would be minimally required
in comparison to you.
The universe was formed after you,
made to resemble your shape,
you give it form as you swim in beauty,
though unaware...
you contain all of God's poetry
written in a single line,
the design of it,
spells out your name.

SWIMMING IN THE RINGS OF SATURN

Our lips play a game
of tug O' war
as they pull
at each other's skin…
in long drawn out
drafts of satisfaction.
I am lost on Vesuvian shores,
as you dive in.
Yesterday we fought over
trivial nothings,
inconsequential in the streams of time
but today,
we make love like gods
swimming in the rings of Saturn.
Our divinity is being reborn
with each kiss,
and crucified with each goodbye.
But no matter how many times I lose you,
or we decide to let go…
I will always find my way home,
which is somewhere between
the moon and the sun,
just west of heaven,
in your arms.

TEMPLES MADE OF WORDS

I've seen something in you that is unseen,
not an eye, or a breast, or anything physically named,
something that for a long time,
has whispered my name, in dreams that I hoped would never end,
I've seen the beginning of the end,
mythic-proportions of timeless-truths,
which all signify forever…
lovers, in love…. forever.
…and we, entangled in what seems to be our own web of destructive-passion,
but actually will save our souls…
that is, our ability to stave off infection of disbelief…
by acknowledging that we were meant to be,
but succumbed to errors of bad timing,
and ingenuity of others…
who sought to keep us apart…
becoming the victims of a God-given-desire…
which lives still,
that we could neither control nor deny,
but only feed with shreds of what time we had together…
which wasn't much, but enough to prevent the starvation of the entity known as
Us…
who has finally awakened from four year sleep,
and hungers once again for what satisfies it best,
the poetry of parted lips wet from words of love…
an ancient language spoken by God's own children,
whose tongues bear witness to his infinite divinity,
by erecting temples made of words,
timeless as Moon, sure as Sun, invisible as Wind,
but real and lasting just the same.
There is a place between heaven and earth…

between dreams and reality,

a place, that when I close my eyes…

I see you as you were meant to be,

with open arms, that beckon me to fall…

…and as I look down the road of our togetherness

I can see, we are at the beginning of a very old end,

which contains more magic and miracles than all legends combined…

because have taken path of poetry…

We are,

Poetry…

THE ALTAR CALLED MY BED

There is old-green-half-melted-candle
which resides at foot of my bed…
and harbors a remembrance of you,
the smell of it reminds me of our togetherness,
and in its flame I can see us making-love.
I still recall buying it…searching for the perfect one…. thinking,
"Can our love last the length of this candle's burning?"
I wanted to defy my destiny (aloneness) and I did, with each lighting of its wick…
but now only a faint aroma of its untimely extinguishment remains…
and the trail of smoke that's left after the outing of every flame,
whose fire burns hotter than can be dreamt of in the hearts of man.
That path of doused burning, that haze of discord,
this line of smoke-trail-goodbyes…
leads me into the not-so-distant past,
when we would take long-hot-showers together….
and wash each other's bodies by the luminosity of our wax-coated-friend,
I see us worshiping one another at the altar-called-my-bed,
with no incense to offer but this candle-named-passion,
whose radiance animates our souls with holy-incandescence.
This is the test by which I measure the worth of all my lovers,
how many candles…how many nights spent burning…
how many kisses-of-forever…
My last lover and I went trough countless wax-aphrodisiacs,
sweating in the love-grip of our inter-dis-course…
watching as the flame disappeared because there was nothing left to burn,
which happens to be true in more ways than can be named…
but you and I have the legacy of not having finished a single one.
This candle resembles the way things ended up with us…
half-done, deformed, green-with-regret,
and so I will place it among all other things that I've left unfinished…

in the past...at my feet...
with the refuse of a-pile-marked-forgotten.
Looks like its time to buy another candle.

THE DARK FACE OF CREATION

What sort of moment is this…
that it can't be captured with words?
Penned to a page
and called poetry…
perhaps it is the
perfect picture of paradise,
it is Adam and Eve
kissing in Eden,
it is you and I
loving in California,
it is the lonely night
making love to the sky
with starry wishes.
You are a vision,
given to a poet
in love with painting
the page poetic
in remembrance of you…
your's is the dark face of creation,
in your eyes is Venus
awaiting her maker…
you lips,
are distant stormy shores
in need of a calm kiss.
What sort of moment is this…
that it can't be captured with words?
It is the invisible touch
of wind on skin,
of lips on cheek,
of me on you…

it is the rings of Saturn,
eternally opulent,
spinning in honor of space
like me…pious poet
writing in honor of you.
It is you and I together
with no better place to be,
than here…among loving looks
and tender touch.

THE END

"You are nothing to me!
You are nothing to me compared to my family!"
You scream
from across what seems to be
a court room drama scene,
but in actuality
is living room floor
suddenly…I don't like it here anymore,
I keep eying the front door,
looking for something more
than a fading feeling
flowing frothily from your face…
finally you say,
"I'm sorry…I'm sorry, please forgive me…"
Oh I see, you think you can just dismiss me
like so much trash waiting to be thrown out
I doubt that you even understand
what it means to stand alone
with no future or home
and roam like a ghost
unloved by most…
Now I drop the bomb,
even my mom
asked me to leave,
cause she never understood me
and that's why we
are in this place
face to face
screaming out meanings
that lack real meaning,

keening, dreaming, leaning
towards saying goodbye
fire on our tongues, tears in our eyes
we die, even as we try to fight
for life amongst all this strife…
and there is no light
at the end of that tunnel,
so quit siphoning my persona
through your mental funnel,
you are not me
never can be
so stop trying to replicate
the gifts that fate
choose to give,
just be kind and live
like you were intended,
because this dichotomy
has just ended,
we broke our hearts
and they can't be mended
we tore a hole
and the rest was rendered
rend, spent
the end.

THE IDEA OF US

I love her…
I mean I barely know her, but I lover her just the same,
not a conventional kind of love,
with birds singing, butterflies in stomach, sleepless nights,
but something in the abstract…
similar to a Jackson Pallock painting
with such a remote-serious-anonymous-ness that its almost mournful,
because I realize she has no idea of my sensibility
(unless of course she does…which isn't likely)
at least she's never let on.
It began with a glance, something in the way she moved, smiled, spoke to me…
captivated my senses, brought them back to life as it were,
then a casual touch, genteel, unforced,
I think we were sitting next to each other on the floor in art class
when she unintentionally brushed against my hand with hers,
reaching past me to grab at some inanimate object
a common-everyday occurrence,
but only to the unseeing eye,
because with that unintentional touch
something began to take place,
something which can't be explained or dissected in modern language,
something so poetic-furious-nameless
that even to write it out in poetry won't do it justice,
(but I'll give it a try anyway…being the poet that I am).
She stuck with me,
again, not in an overt way, but with subtle grace,
and since then,
in my mind's eye, she makes herself ready,
we laugh, talk, write, create together,
works of art contained in conversation…

Oblivious to my imaginary-delights she randomly asks me a question,
about what kind of wood was used in a certain project,
I answer in kind, but inwardly, am dying to touch her hand again…just once,
to feel the sturdy grip of possibility,
and know the joy of her skin intimately.
Everyone has that someone that they wonder about from time to time,
but never have the courage or disposition to go near…
she is my someone,
I think I am in love, not so much with her,
but mostly…with the idea of us,
of what could be, but never will…
life is so sad.

THE LOVE I'VE LOST LOVING YOU

How many nights did we spend making love under moonlight…
With nothing to cover our nakedness, but night's air…
when you were still shy, and afraid that someone might see us
acting like, "wild animals" in the park.
How many moans of pleasure came from your mouth sounding like my name…
As we inhale-and-exhale, with me inside of you…and you on top of me,
sweating through the intercourse, which would become our demise.
How many times have our tongues tasted each other…
and our lips caressed, as the wine evaporated off our breath…
You always loved me best when you were drunk,
so well in fact, that I would say,
"Thank God for alcohol…"
after we'd made love, and we would laugh in the darkness.
Lately though…despite all of our togetherness,
you have the nerve to act as though you've never known me in that way…
Causing me to remember with tender-angry-sadness
the-love-I've-lost-loving-you,
and I think,
"If only I had known how things would end up, maybe…"
Maybe what?
Maybe I'd have done things differently?
The truth is…
I've always known how things would become between you and I after the fall,
but I held on anyway…you see, I wanted to defy fate…
and I was satisfied with giving destiny a sucker-punch,
knowing full well,
that I could never defeat an opponent, whose reach spans the length of time.
So, I mostly remember the way things were…
and wish that I could exist in that moment between then and now,
when tomorrow was still a possible forever,

and all our yesterdays were the tears-we-could-not-escape…
Still…I've come to learn,
no matter how much you try to avoid the past…
it has a way of finding you…
in the future.

THE MAGIC OF ECLIPSE

The Moon fell in love with the Sun,
but alas, day and night cannot occupy the same space…
thus was born Twilight,
that place of in-betweens,
neither dark nor light,
forever-Sunset-Moonrise.
And now in the Sun's burning orb
there remains evidence of Moon's blue smile,
crescent of passionate Moon-kiss…
reminding Sun of its own divinity.
Moon too has become brighter from knowing Sun
and vowed to shine upon all loving Moon-gazers
in the name of Midnight.
But only when Sun and Moon kiss in Heaven's sight
can we know the magic of Eclipse.
Good night fair Moon,
may you know no lover like the Sun.

THE NAKED WRITTEN YOU

I see you there, writing your poetry with mad-crazy-passion…
intently, you twist your sentences together until they resemble:
your anger…your loss…your grief…
I watch you write a line,
mouthing the words to see if they fit.
Fiercely gripping your pen, guarding that book of yours,
as if it contained secrets of the world…
and it does.
Somehow I think you are a prophet of your own inclination,
writing out truths that most will never know,
because they're to busy murdering themselves with complacency…
and while the world around you is burning-alive,
you just keep on writing.
I think you are trying to write yourself into oblivion,
perhaps by verbalizing your pain…you will finally escape it,
and if nothing else, you will have a record of your wrongs,
something that reminds you of all your sins, and why you are paying for them.
And as I write of you, I wonder…if you ever write about me,
but are to afraid to admit it.
Or if…maybe, somewhere in those unintentional moments of clarity,
when your hand is tired from writing,
but you mind is still full of poetry…
do you think of me?
Because sometimes, when our minds are arguing,
our eyes are in complete agreement,
I get the sense that you know me…
or at least, I think…you want to.
Still, as presumptuous as this may sound,
I want to know you too,
and all the words that make you who you are…

seeing the naked-written-you.
Also, bearing my-metaphoric-self to your soul,
all the while...
enlarging the poem-of-us.
After all, isn't this what poetry is all about?
Wait...don't answer that...
just keep on writing.

IN THE SILENCE OF A CROWDED ROOM

I manage to say with brokenness…
"I'm sorry…for everything, I'm sorry…"
and watch with eager eyes for your slightest reaction,
hoping to see some semblance of the love we once shared,
of stolen-nights spent in each other's arms,
kissing-holding-touching-laughing-crying-looking-ahead
to the day when we knew we would go our separate ways.
I remember telling you,
"I never want to speak to you again, you no longer exist to me,
I have thrown away all our correspondence, you should do the same…"
lies that I wrote to set Us free,
because I knew that the only way we would ever fulfill our respective-destinies
would be when we said goodbye…
And in these next few seconds of remembrance,
while I wait for your response to my clumsy-apology,
I seem to recall a hundred nights of our togetherness,
tender-moments, spent in a quiet bedroom, over looking the ocean,
priceless expressions-of-affection,
when we looked into each other's eyes for days at a time,
with nothing better to do,
than smile at one another in the silence…
you have been, and always will be, my one-true-love.
"I'm sorry too, for everything…" you say delicately,
and in voice of tender-forgiveness,
bringing me back to this awkward-apologetic-moment,
We nod in the silence-of-now-and-always,
while those around us are laughing-talking-shaking-hands
and I think,
There is nothing in the world so important as this second,
when I can finally conclude the tragedy of us,

by telling you goodbye the way I was supposed to,
and as you walk away from me,
child-in-arm, face glowing, looking casually over your shoulder,
I realize that I never stopped loving you…not for a second,
I only managed to ignore the inescapable truth,
that you were my destiny, and I blew it…
because I was too blind to see how rich I had become
by sharing in the treasure of you…
and tomorrow, as I prepare to see you for the last time,
I sense that I will be mostly remembering the past,
the days when you held my hand like you loved me,
and when our kisses contained the promise of forever…
I will be loving you in the silence of a crowded room,
among strangers, whose laughter makes no sense to me,
not when something as precious as our love is on the line,
and whose heart's may never feel the completion of their souls,
by the touch of another,
Perhaps this is what it means to know peace at last…
accepting loss, moving on, coping with regret,
after all, tears never were an adequate way of crying,
and laughter can't even compare
to the way I felt when I was with you…
whole…complete…alive…
with no where better to be,
than in your presence.

THE TREE OF OUR TOGETHERNESS

I passed that tree again today…remember?
The one where we made love under a full moon,
not far from lonely stretch of American highway.
Its branches bent in the wind…
and I couldn't help but think of that night,
the silhouette of you clutching the bark,
while I pushed myself deeper inside you.
I realize of course,
that you are embarrassed to be reminded of such things,
but there are some moments that I cannot forget…
the image of them, burned in my memory.
Like the sacred look on your face when we first kissed,
in an overcrowded airport, amongst strangers,
or the sight of us covered in hay, as we wrestled in your uncle's barn…
so young and full of mischief.
We were always in love, but just couldn't admit it…
I remember traveling across country in that tiny car of yours,
laughing-crying-kissing all the way to California,
and thinking that we could finally be together,
like we were supposed to be…
only, that's not what happened,
our souls were at odds, and the light of what once was,
became a darkness that we could not escape.
My anger-your tenderness, my courage-your fear, my pain-your love…
these were the everyday issues of our togetherness,
and the bitter chords of our untimely demise.
Just last night you came to see me perform,
in the crowd you sat anonymously, and by the dim stage light,
I noticed that you cut your hair…it looked good, it looked like you,
before we were together, and before all our misery,

when we could still smile.
When the show was over I called your name
as you tried to sneak out back door unseen,
I embraced you and said, "Thanks for coming..."
and you gave me a half-hug,
but I was glad just to feel you near me again, and I thanked God for this...
for being able to see you...to drink in your smile...
to feel your skin touching mine...
and as you walked away, I made a holy wish in my heart,
that you and I would regain our composure, let go of the past,
forget the pain, and move on...
then, in milliseconds of prophetic-vision
I think I saw the future, or at least what could be.
We sat alone in a room-full-of-smiles,
and with shades drawn...our souls kissed,
not in a romantic way, but with forgiving-restoration,
then we laughed till dawn,
you stood at my wedding,
among my dearest and most trusted friends,
and again we laughed.
This is our maybe-destiny,
to be the pall-bearers of a dead-and-gone good-bye,
and to usher in a new era of possible-hello-laughing-tomorrows,
yet beyond this prophecy remains something unforgettable...that tree...
The tree of our togetherness.

THE WORLD IS OUR BEDROOM

We make love spontaneously…
in front of mirrors, over sinks, behind closed doors,
wherever…whenever…whatever…
skin on skin, touching through clothes,
casual interaction of two lovers,
we smile…and dance the dance of our brother-Father the Sun,
and our sister-Mother the Moon…
sometimes it begins with a kiss…or a touch,
senses come alive and it's on!
I'm on top, she's on top,
or were both upside down in some awkward position…
just so long as it feels good,
just so long as I can make her cum…like she has never cum before,
and she tells me this to my face, with eager lips that speak thankfully, she says,
"Before I met you I was convinced that a man would never make me cum…"
she was wrong…I give her profound-spiritual-orgasms…
she equates me with God in her screams and moans,
"yes…yes…yes…oh-God-baby-yes…that's it…yes!!!"
I smile…and feel like true man,
or more so like a lover who is good at loving…
and I know she feels this too,
she respects me for my ability to make her feel
like the ultimate-woman without being the typical-male.
We take my motorcycle every chance we get…
and in the mountains, among animals, we speak of making love,
the world is our bedroom…
no curtains to hide us from the eyes of others, we are unabashedly free,
and figure…why hide
when we are seen by God in everything we purpose to do anyway?
When she spreads her legs I see my home,

that soft fold of pink-fleshy-tissue…
its wet-warm-invitation of open lips and promised delight,
she says, "I want you to come inside…"
as if I have been psychically away from home
and am standing just outside her front door,
I like this, I am in love with the idea of "coming inside" she is home to me,
her arms form the gate of welcome-and-never-have-to-leave…
she is my constellation,
her illumination guides my way through this otherwise starless night-called-life.
We sleep together most nights on a fold-out-couch,
she is always cold, I am always hot…
she is always day, I am always night…
and in this paradox there is truth,
relentless-friendly-speculative-ordinary-truth
not revelatory, but honest, quiet, sincere in its unobtrusiveness…
it says with a one-winked-eye, and cocky-jaded-smile
"…yes…"
that's all…nothing more…
and I think I understand,
what more can be said that could possibly describe our love in better terms,
what more than yes…
nothing more…
yes.

THE YOU I WANT

There are poems that I have written:
about you…for you…because of you…
but never given to you,
you seem to exist outside of all that,
unconsciously defying my every intent,
by making love a game,
whose rules apply to only yourself.
You once asked a friend of mine if he thought I was,
"capable of love…"
He said, "Yes…. very much so…"
and you replied by uttering,
"Hmmmm…" with raised eyebrows,
as if in disbelief, that I knew what I was saying,
when I said,
'I love you…'
and you told me to,
'sleep on it…'
Perhaps it is you who are incapable of loving someone,
because you are to hung up on your past,
or to afraid to face your future…
and maybe its a combination of both
that prevents you from knowing true love.
Stop running from me every time I ask you for a little intimacy,
afraid that if we touch,
you might lose it…let down your guard…
begin to feel something for someone other than yourself…
acting as though you don't want to know me in that way,
if that's the case,
you sure have a funny way of showing it,
by spreading your legs, and pulling me on top of you…

because I whispered in your ear…
Is that what you call not wanting someone?
Then, it occurs to me…I must not want you either,
only the idea of you…
because that's all you really are to me,
an image…. something that I've placed on a pedestal,
so that I can admire it from a distance…
and say to my friends,
"See what I posses…ain't she lovely, I made her myself…"
because the you I want,
is only a figment of my imagination,
someone I've conjured up,
so that I won't have to exist alone.
I realize now of course…its better to be alone,
than to fool myself into thinking,
I could ever have anything real with you…
at least alone, is something I can feel.

THINK OF WE

…when you think of all the good things in this lifetime,
when you think of sunshine
like shafts through trees,
and breezes on hot summer days,
when you think of moon beams on lovers backs in midnight,
when you think of candlelight,
fire light,
no light…
and the possibilities that they carry,
think of me and my possible selves,
think of how we embody each other completely,
think of madness and laughter,
think of sky and ocean,
think of universe and god,
think of me,
think of we.

THIS NIGHT FOREVER

Magical moments slipping away,
melting into memories…
like silent raindrops falling,
softly…we kiss.
Tender affections of an unexpected friendship,
caressing body and soul…
drinking in the beauty of yourself,
I whisper a song,
capturing the present,
reliving the past…
freeze framing this night forever.
Remembering now, each touch of our lips…
passion pouring over,
holding you, tightly…
like a lost treasure.
Laughing, talking, sharing everything…
tow innocent children,
without regret we give and take,
sensual exchanges.
Leaving now?
Take me with you…
my heart will say.
You are gone, and still I hear your laughter
echoing in the corridors of my mind.

TO BE LOVED

This day began
with remembrances
of our laughter,
pieces of you and I
reserved for today's journey.
They line my mind
like memory drapes
reminding me of who we are
when we are alone
in the purity of night,
with only kisses
to communicate
our togetherness…
which is the only truth
to be found
for miles in this
universe of lies…
I smile,
say your name
quietly to myself
and remember
how holy you are to me
my saint sage,
a prayer brought to life…
given skin to be touched
lips to be kissed
a heart to be loved.
Amen.

To Finally Kiss Poetry At Last

"You remind me of a movie that I've never seen,
but am now watching again for the first time."
She says simply, and I think,
"How fitting, that she knows my poetry…
before she's even had a chance to read it…"
that's an omen, a blessed sign of our togetherness,
which implies that sentience is just around the corner.
"I've been looking my whole life for a poet…
who'll make sweet love to me, and give me poetry."
she remarks purposeful, and I say to myself,
'Looks like I came just in time…'
Then we dance, slow tender dance of possibilities in her living room,
bare-foot, music touchingly serenading our ears,
as we stare at each other in long moments of true passion.
Then I have unwise desire to talk, and ask, "So…what's next?"
Hoping to hear her say, 'next we make love…'
but instead, she looks at me with small-genteel-smile and says,
"Now…I will always wonder what it could have been like…"
"What do you mean?"
I ask, dumbfounded that she's so soon sick of me,
she just stares with sad-somber eyes,
"But we've only just begun…"
I plead, to no avail, she's made up her mind,
sees dismal future of our hearts being broken for one-another,
decides this is not worth the risk, and tells me goodbye on the spot.
I gather my things, (which have been strewn throughout apartment)
head towards door…she says at last second,
"Wait…don't leave things like this…" I stop just short of door and say,
"You're a coward! You talk big, but deep down, your afraid of getting hurt…
I can respect your fears,

but I can't respect your choice to let them get the best of you, the best of Us..."

She explains that this is right thing for her, telling me,

"There's no room for anyone but you in your life...

you don't need anybody, just your poetry..."

and I think, 'Wish poetry were a woman...that I could kiss her lips...'

(random poetic thought) all the while, she persists,

I listen, but shake head in disagreement...and that's when I say,

"Are you sure? Absolutely positive,

that you want to say goodbye to me, goodbye to poetry...

This is the last time I'm going to ask you...don't...do...this..."

Then in moment of sudden giving-in, she bursts into hugs and kisses,

saying "all right...all right...all right..." as if relieved,

satisfied that I stayed long enough for her to change unchangeable female mind.

We kiss, dance a while longer, then make our way to her bed,

where we establish the beginning of our poetry,

then I leave, go home, to empty bed and think,

I stayed, when it would have been so easy to just walk out door,

I stayed...because I see poetry in her eyes,

feel poetry in her lips,

and know now what it means,

to finally kiss poetry at last.

TO TOUCH THE SKY

...so here we are among God and sky,
in some unexpected poetic moment
of laughter and all alone,
which has its birth in the second we said hello,
and finds its completion right here and now
in the liquid voice of waterfalls.
I've always wanted to touch the sky,
and in being with you,
I feel I've done that.
...because hidden away somewhere in that brilliant burning smile of yours
is a sadness I cannot begin to know,
only recognize as sister to my own pain.
...because misunderstanding is a monster
whose teeth have tasted us both,
only we've managed to escape
the verbal knives thrown at us by would be friends,
by not forgetting who we are as individuals.
...and I think that while you were looking away,
perhaps at some random fallen leaf caught in the brook,
I heard the mountain say a secret to my soul...it said,
"This one is sister to the sun, which is your brother and father to us all."
and I smile unseen smile in the corner of my mouth,
because am now acutely aware of your soul's burning,
which is a kin to my own,
we are siblings of the sun.
...and as we sit silent on sentient stones
of Indian origin,
I write this poem in my mind,
musing with myself on whether or not
you'd appreciate its meaning

were I to deliver it to your ear…
…so as you shine
I write,
and together we walk
along stolen trails of our fathers forgotten past
understanding what it means at last
to touch the sky.

TOMORROW WILL BE A BETTER DAY

Last night I caught a butterfly in your honor,
it was my intent to let it go when we met
as a symbol of our love for one another…
token of kisses wet with wings,
but sadly this was not what occurred,
instead, by the time I got home,
the butterfly was half dead,
and we were at odds…
sad circumstance of too much work
and not enough time alone,
to enjoy the company of candy caress.
…and now Marvin Gaye is singing softly
like a poet in background,
"let's make love tonight, cause we do it right, sexual healing…"
and I bob my head to the tune of this,
knowing that there is much forgiveness in a touch,
and even more tenderness in a look
of complete and utter love,
which is the only way I can see you
as you sleep next to me
on this cold California night,
I kiss your forehead, and say
"sleep my love…"
knowing that we cannot,
because have too many words between us,
and so must lie awkwardly awake
staring at ceiling fan,
tumbling in bed like ghosts…
hoping quietly in our hearts

that tomorrow
will be a better day.

TOO MANY WORDS...

...still I wonder what it was about the break up that hurt me so?

I think is was the image of you with another lover,

not just another man...

(that I could have dealt with)

but a lover, tender forever's whispered to each other in darkness

holding him, kissing him, loving him like you did me...

this...and the awful feeling of guttural uncertainty

which came with our lengthy-departure from one another's lives,

because, to be honest...

I figured it'd last longer than it did,

(It being of course, the illusion of love)

in-fact, I never thought It would end,

but It did, and so did We...

We ended the night We first kissed,

the night when I looked in your eyes

and saw an eerie reflection of our eventual demise

in the shape of my own blurry image,

the night you told me I was "The One"

the night true-love died from inconsistency

and security gave way to incompleteness.

This was our sad new-beginning of goodbye and unable to cope

of too many miserable-hang-ups to deal with

of angry words shot like bullets from our gun-mouths

(aimed at the heart)

you hanging by a thread of sanity,

and me glaring insanely at you from across the room...

I kept telling you to leave...but you wouldn't, you kept holding onto thin air,

I've never seen anything like it...

the way you loved me so enduringly,

with propriety and decency,

and all the things that make for a successful relationship,

you loved me, you loved me…

but not enough, or perhaps too much.

Then…("then" which always seems to strike like lightening)

when I'd become comfortable with the idea of us

confident in our union of supposed-forever,

you were fed-up, quit, out the door

and on the back of someone else's motorcycle.

…and I am sad for the loss of you,

unhappy miserable day that you left me wanting you, and since your departure,

not a single moment has occurred without thoughts of you, thoughts of Us and
what if…

words which come to mind inexpressible-fractured-incomplete

words, words, words…

are all I have left to remember you by,

and why I lost you in the first place.

Too many words…

TRANCE

We dance dance dance,
in midnight trance
of naked and no pants…
under moon and stars,
Red face of Mars
making amends
as we sin
like sinners
in love with sin…
let's begin
at the end
and end with friends
or let's not end
only begin
in this never ending beginning…
because we are transcending
the first phase of normalcy
because in love with beats
and poetry, the un-definable we
that is you and I,
shooting stars in sky…
looking like love in eyes
and I say under days demise,
"Every time I see you, a star is falling…"
perhaps this is our calling,
to be falling ourselves
it's half past twelve,
and all I can taste is you
like human sugar cube
sweet on lips,

what a trip
as we dip into flesh
our bodies mesh
no stress, only bless-ings
of coming, and going
knowing the never before known
poem of you and I
sweet lullaby of lovers cry…
ooohhh mmmyyy,
my my my my my my goodness
my god, my goddess
undressed, and blessed…
forget sex…
as we trance and
dance dance dance,
trance.

UNDER QUILTS AND CANDLES

"Are you close to cuming?"
"I'm close to becoming…" she says.
…and then we dive in for more,
more flesh, more sex,
more of this unbelievable feeling
of complete and utter satisfaction.
I ask, "What does it feel like to have me inside you…"
and she says, "It feels like a cloud."
…and now I know
what it means to fly
without the notion of wings,
but on a bed of pure
golden ecstasy
called womb and man
made in a miracle moment
of heaven meets hell…
they fall in love
and now the world will know
that there is no sin
in making love,
no sin in being who we are,
in doing what we do,
as nature has seen fit
to give us guidance.
There is only beauty here,
only skin being kissed,
only souls being exchanged…
only us in love
finding our divinity
under quilts

and candlelight…
but finding.

UNDER THE SPELL OF WATER

Somewhere among the relics of last night's love affair…
in-between breaths of "…hold me and never let go…"
I seem to recall what it was like to belong,
momentary-misgivings-of-a-mad-poet
whose idea of being in love…. is having a lover like you to call his own,
and I think I remember hearing you say,
"I'm glad we finally found each other…"
and I responded with tender-intent,
"Now the trick is making it work…"
because we both know that "love" never lasts…at least not in our worlds,
where marriage is synonymous with suicide,
and the wedding band, as you so poignantly put it, represents a "hand-cuff"
not a gold-band which indicates the circle of eternity,
and supposedly the nature of marital-commitment…
when it is actually something far more sterile and unforgiving,
so we agree to be lovers-of-the-living-kind…
instead of limiting ourselves to the potential "contract"
of a maybe-dead-marriage…
where nothing ever seems to work out, and all parties involved, eventually become
callous to the art-of-passion,
and in fact, I think that we cannot help but be otherwise,
…kissing you, was as natural as taking a breath…
gentle familiar un-refrained longing
playful, innocent…
like two children exploring the wilderness of each other's eyes,
we laugh-kiss-moan-breath in unison.
I tell you, "…so much poetry is happening right now…"
and I sense that you feel the same,
you never said so (you didn't have to) at least not verbally,
but in wordless looks of concurrence…

which speaks more meaning to me
than anything you might have thought to say in response.
So…Art became Poetry,
and vice-versa, as we sat upright-and-naked in your bed…
legs wrapped together in symbiotic position,
listening to The Doors, and agreeing that our song would be, "The End"
Morrison's infamous soliloquy of torn lovers…angry-discontent-rantings of a
dispossessed child…who has gone Oedipus.
A wonderful premise to build any relationship on…wouldn't you say?
Finally…we make our way to the shower…that wet place of infinity,
where we caressed one another in the soft-light of 5am…
and kissing you…under the spell of water,
I am reminded of what it means to taste the soul of another,
whose essence is as ancient as my own…
This was one of those nights that we'll never forget,
and many years from now, when we're dying in our beds…
we'll look back on this time with tears in our eyes…
and smiles on our faces…all because we took a chance,
letting our hearts have their way,
while our lips took the stage.

UNIVERSE ENOUGH FOR ME

We are opposing planets you and I…
aligning in some prophetic moment,
revolving on an axiom of celestial-love.
In this millennial passing of ours,
we leave behind a wake of star-gazers…
they watch us from their fragile-empty-worlds.
We look to them like:
two brilliant satellites,
blazing in the dark loneliness of their never ending night.
And with our god-like-selves,
we inspire them to dream,
secret dreams of cosmic rendezvous,
and falling stars.
And by the light of our togetherness,
they look for someone to kiss,
but not with their lips…
with their soul.
Because by looking up to see our beauty,
they must look back down and see their aloneness.
And so we become a part of the poetry,
that every lover writes for another…
and in doing so we live forever side by side,
if not in the heavens,
then in the hearts and music,
of every living creature that has witnessed our union.
And in the orbit of our lives,
perhaps we will pass this way again…
only closer, so that I may touch you again,
in a more magical way than before.

For you are my eternal-beloved,
and your eyes contain universe enough for me.

WAIT FOR ME

You remind me of that feeling I get,
just before I fall asleep,
warm, inviting, comfortable.
I am thinking of you now,
and will be for some time.
Wait for me there,
in that secret place
called dreams…
We'll share a kiss or two
and pass a time
in each other's hearts
unaware of the approaching day.
We'll laugh,
run through fields of gold,
and be lazy on clouds.
Then we'll make
our way back home
to a house that we've built
with our own two minds.
Yawn,
sleep,
we.

WE ARE

We are the keepers of a lost art you and I...
writers of thoughts and words left unspoken,
our powers of creation lie on the tips of our tongues,
and the points of our pens.
We are the makers of a sacred text,
whose poetry has been forgotten,
and whose meaning is as timeless as life itself,
with a sanctity and a significance
which defies all.
We are the ageless parody of youth
with our dreams in one hand,
and our heart in the other...
we go though life searching,
but never fully understanding.
We are the travelers of a never ending journey,
our quest is to find a treasure of immortal rhyme,
the soliloquy of eternal truth,
for in these unearthed songs of our spirit
we find serenity.
We are the journalists of experience...
ever recording our memories
always expressing our feelings on paper,
and thus we escape.
This is what we are,
what we were meant to be,
and what we cannot escape.

WE ARE LOST

Last Monday
you filled my tank with gas,
so that we could make it last
a few more miles…
this Monday
you left my heart empty with goodbye,
sad senseless so long.
I watched you from my rear view mirror
as I drove away
on half a tank of love,
you wandered sadly to the door of our
ocean beach bungalow,
and in that lingering moment
of I love you
and all alone…
we are lost.

WE BELONG

I can think of a thousand reasons why it won't work:
love is a lie…time is the great antecedent to all falsehoods…
we're both used to being alone…
just to name a few,
but one reason over rides all of this heinous bull-shit,
I feel it…
not with my brain, but in my soul,
in the very molecules that make up my existence,
I know that we are meant to be…
if not for all time, then right here and now,
while we're alive and can be together…
among the discards of past lovers and future selves
which lay strewn in the essence-of-unpredictability,
we are destined to paint our love on poetic-canvas-of-immutability,
because while the world changes around us, we remain basically the same…
in love, despite scars that won't heal, and wounds that continue to bleed,
we will survive.
Some idiot once wrote that,
"…if you truly love something, let it go,
and if it was meant to be yours it will come back to you…"
what a crock,
if you truly love something you never hold it captive in the first place,
that's not love, that's control, that's blind-self-aggression,
holding something so tightly that you kill it,
and contaminate your own soul in the process,
I can no more hold you than I can hold the stars,
you shine far too brightly, and besides…
I want to see your beauty as I stand beside you,
not on top of you…
your artistry inspires me because it contains all the aspects of magical-you,

and perhaps a few traits that I envy as well…
I recognize your autonomous-self, and declare my own independence…
we are separate…. never to make up two halves of the same whole,
but rather, two wholes of the same pair…
complete unto ourselves, but more spectacular together…
as lovers, as artist, as souls caught in the void,
we compliment…not replace, we give…not order, we love…not control,
because we are secure in our aloneness,
and we realize that the only other person we could never be without,
is each other…
feeling something is far better than thinking it…
because my mind has never been true to me,
but my soul guides me in the direction of destiny…
right here to this portion of hallowed ground,
our bed of holy-new-beginnings
you and I…
we are meant to be,
and for the first time in my life
I know what it's like to come home,
and belong,
we belong.
Say it with me…
and tell me if it fits in your mouth as well as it does mine,
We…belong.
Yes! Yes!! Yes!!!

WE SHINE

What are you doing?
I'm building something in my mind…
as we climb
to the top
of this love rock,
and that's the spot
at the very top
where we'll rock
each other's socks off.
On this 4000 foot drop off,
steeper than time
as we unwind
and find
the time
to be kind,
just you and I,
with ravens in sky
of this mountain high night.
Oh, and that's right,
we brought along
a love song
in the form of tiny little dog
who has followed us along
this long and winding trial,
like a love letter in the mail
seen but unsent
or better yet sent but unseen
as we make our way through a scene
of green and trees
counting these

elevated footsteps
like promises being kept
as we leap or should I say leapt
into a day of dreams that dreamt
without being slept.
We're left to the devices of time,
as we climb, climb, climb
rhyme into each other's souls
taking a hold
of each fragmented piece
until we feel the peace
and sweet release
of you on me
we on knees
among these sage trees,
and summer breeze
we laugh with such ease,
attempting to please
our primal desires
white hot fires
that burn in our minds
as we grind, and climb,
and attempt to unwind
our minds to find
the time, we came to find,
sublime, love of mine
you shine, I shine
we shine.

WHAT IT MEANS TO BE LOVERS

2 a.m. on old fold out couch,
and we are wet from watery kisses,
your legs spread,
and I see the light for first time
radiating between your chocolate thighs,
as we swim among cinnamon consummation
and milky dreams.
Here is an almost forgotten poem,
rescued from the depths of memory.
Liquid lips as we swallow each other's souls,
piece by delicious piece...
I softly kiss every inch of you,
whisper secret poems in your ear,
worshiping your skin with my tongue,
until you come freely to that place where we belong...
as you moan in the dark,
I belong to the night,
which is you wet with desire,
as we bathe ourselves in golden candlelight.
...and now we hide like children
under tangled cotton feather sheets
that conceal our purple togetherness...
until at last we lay motionless,
spent...spinning, unable to move
from our loss of gravity,
having exhausted all the possibilities
of our nocturnal love,
and your skin is speaking darkly to me,
now I know the true beauty of night,
which is you, and you know true poetry

which is what it means...
to be lovers.

WHEN YOU SMILE

Your right eye
is a little darker than your left,
which reminds me of fall,
cloudy October skies
that break into midnight…
and so I bring you leaves
from the basement of time,
gathered in the name
of forever.
Looking to the cold
California night
I kick a star…
and notice that
even the moon
in all her glowing
doesn't own half
as much divinity as you
when you smile…

WONDERWALL

And the song says,
"Maybe, your gonna' be the one that saves me…
cause after all…you're my Wonder-wall…"
and I take comfort in that,
the thought that perhaps there is someone out there that can save me…
prevent me from my crash-n-burn-cycle of life.
Someone who can help heal the tragic-wounds of my past,
by: wiping away my tears…kissing my lips…easing my pain…
As I mouth the words, visualizing you with each breath…I laugh.
Because I realize that for me…
there is more love in holding your hand, than in all the sex in the world,
and somehow…standing silent in your presence, just being near you,
makes life more meaningful.
And if you are as you say, "Like an old pair of jeans…"
then so you are,
comfortable…full of character…a perfect fit…
and let me never wear another pair, as long as you are in my life,
because none suits me so well as you.
And the song says,
"I don't believe that any body…feels the way I do…about you now…"
and its true,
you are my Wonderwall…and the crazy thing is, you know it…
you know that with your kiss you make my sadness disappear,
you know that by holding my hand you cause me to relive lost-dreams.
Still you remain elusive….
because I just don't do it for you,
I can't be the person that you've always wanted…because of my sins….
because of all the erotic poetry that is stacked under my bed,
and because it is my self-fulfilling-prophecy to be alone.
And the song says,

"All the roads that lead your there are winding...
and all the lights that light the way are blinding..."
and I go numb with the chorus...
because it represents everything that can never be,
two poets lost in a sea of life-maddening-thoughts,
to busy for romance, and to afraid of what destiny might say...
but fate has never been good to me, and my entire life has been a raw deal.
And the song says,
"There are many things that I would like to say to you, but I don't know how..."
and I cry at that,
because I know that no matter what I say,
I can never say enough...to bring you to me,
all I can do is hit the repeat button...
manage through the chorus...
and hope for the best....

YOU DELIVER ME

Sometimes we kiss
and your lips are cold
from having been licked
and blown by the wind.
It reminds me of sweet honeydew melon
on a thick summer afternoon,
after having worked all day in the sun.
You are the treasure that I come home to,
the reason I come home at all,
in your womb, your heart, your soul
is all the heaven I will ever need,
and it delivers me
you deliver me.

You Look Like Poetry

Sneaking in your room on a lonely 4am morning,
whispering...I say, "I need you to hold me..."
and you do, without hesitation you reach out to me,
with your hands you ease my pain,
never opening your eyes, you tell me that you love me,
and holding you in the darkness, in this moment,
I am convinced that I can't let you go,
not before I tell you how I feel.
Sitting here on the edge of your bed, and on the brink of loving,
running my fingers through your hair, watching you sleep,
I lean over, and gently kiss your forehead,
"Good night..." I say, and secretly I hope for a thousand more.
More nights that begin and end just like this one,
with me kissing your cheek, while you hold my hand.
I ask God for this, for one good-night with you,
holding you in the warmth of our togetherness,
while we speak in the conversation-of-pure-silence.
Smiling, I pull the covers over you again,
making sure you're warm,
and as I turn to leave, abandoning the idea of us,
I realize...these were five of the happiest-minutes-of-my-life,
but in the morning they will be only a vague memory to you.
And so the dream-of-us is lost to insomnia,
a sleep-less-ness of the soul,
caused by prolonged wanting of you.
I have lived lifetimes in your eyes,
tender-sleepy-moments-of-I-love-you-and-forever,
and from where I stand...you look like poetry.
The irony of it is that tomorrow
when I tell you all of this,

you will look at me as though I've lost my mind…
and instead of embracing me, you will not know what to feel.
In the days to come I will call-and-write you,
with the poem of us, long-distance-what-if's-and-why-not's,
hearing for the first time,
an awkward replacement to the easy-give-and-take of our laughter.
All the poetic-words-in-the-world could never do you justice,
and as hard as I try I can't verbalize the vision of you…
The infinite tragedy of it all is that I will have lost you
before I really had a chance to know you,
and on some destined night, we will meet in San Francisco,
and I will still be sleepless from my desire,
but with a book full of poetry,
written to resemble you.

BY THE WAY...WHO ARE YOU?

I tell you how attracted I am,
you say,
"I'm not going to sleep with you..."
and I remember thinking,
"Man...I wish she hadn't said that..."
because as soon as those words left your mouth,
I knew we'd be in bed by the end of the night...
and sure enough,
we were.
By the way...
who are you?

LOST ANGELS

We gathered rocks and sage from the basement of California,
as we walked along lotus paths of the Angeles trails,
lost among images of waterfalls,
winding raging creeks,
and silent pools of perfection
juxtaposed to a steep cliff face
that seemed to contain elements of our ancestry.
Our lunch, hiding like a secret in brown paper bags
as we march to our inevitability,
two lonely poets of each other,
writing our love like madness being felt
with kisses and screams.
No words, just the rhythmic breathing
of our enamors endeavors
to conquer the continuous climb of today's amore.
I carry our food like a child on my back,
holding it delicately above the cold clear waters,
as my brow perspires possibility,
and we make our way from here to there,
and then back to over here
for what seems like years,
but is actually only a few happy hours
passed like lemonade on hot summer days
in a hammock of shade and imagination.
This mountain is like our life together,
beautiful, dangerous, cold,
emanating complete safety,
but treacherous at times...
I keep stubbing my toes on the large grey rocks
that line our paths, and think,

sometimes it hurts to be in love
with an angel of tragedy…
which you are,
a glowing moon of my desire…
steeped in resilience
but we trounce on,
in the direction of the rising sun,
over pains and pockets of pre-emancipation
that drips down our lonely skins,
in the form of shared waters
making us thirsty with laughter and suns.
We keep smiling at the leaves
and reminding each other that
there is only a little daylight left,
so we must hurry home
for a hot bath in candlelight
and memory making that is more like
god creating, or recapturing our divinity
two lost angels
in Los Angeles
alone,
and in love.

FOR HAVING BEEN

Look at all the pretty flowers
that decorate our roads
like children in the field…
they remind me of you and I
driving across country
in an effort to reclaim our sanity.
You the saint,
I the madman,
and the road, our poetry.
How divine it was to be young
and in love with life,
in love with ourselves,
in love with the idea of each other…
like nomads on the move to secret places.
so too did we own the world before us.
I sit now, vaguely remembering
those days with a distant feeling of sadness
for all the nights spent groping in the darkness
of our untimely departure…
still, for all the pains it has caused me,
I am better for having known,
we are eternally better
for having been.

LIKE THE CHILDREN WE ARE

Have you ever seen such a dawning…
as the one you are bearing witness to right now?
Which is me inside of you,
and you on top of me,
tangled in the strands of midnight,
falling all about the bed
like drum beats hitting the ear,
soft low hum of bass breaths
being breathed in the stillness,
eagerly anticipating each glowing motion
with such cool jeweled comfort…
that when we are done,
all that is left
are the echoes of I love you's
whispered between kisses,
and the nocturnal
madness, melting into
wax of our spilled candles,
we laugh, and fall asleep
clumsily forgetting the fights we've had
in exchange for the dreams we'll have
and together we glow
like the children we are.

KISSED SUCKED BITTEN AND CARESSED

So here I am again,
dangling between Venus and Saturn,
kissing two women at the same time
on a moonlit California midnight
full of wine, full of weed, full of ecstasy…
full of life and a face full of skin.
I do not know,
nor do I care
what other men might believe
about the opposite sex,
because I know now at last
that they are indeed divine,
that their lips are sentient,
that their breasts are magic moons,
that their honeycomb is sweet and alive.
I have fallen in love today,
with the entire female population,
with their sex, their madness, their matriarchy…
al-ohm, which in Arabic means mother,
ohm…the universal sound of harmony,
ohm, the first syllable of womanhood,
I meditate on it like a monk facing pre-enlightenment,
I toss it around with my tongue,
let the sound of it settle like taste in my mouth.
Ooohhhmmmm,
wwwooommmaaannn…
ooohhhmmm.
I am a saint by osmosis,
my soul has been saved by the sanctity of milk,
the power of long lashes

and glowing eyes,
of licked lips and candlelight…
of being kissed, sucked, bitten, and caressed.
I have seen heaven,
it resides on the inner thigh
of every woman in the world…
they carry it like a secret waiting to be shared,
like a child waiting to be had,
like a moment waiting to be lived.
I give myself to the goddess,
worship at the temple female,
make amends for the sins of man
committed in ignorance
against the soul of woman,
I am lost, I am found,
I am upside down.

BEING MADE HOLY

Last night I rubbed knees with the gods,
on andalusian promises of freedom,
I lay spinning…lost somewhere between
the gravity of Venus and Saturn,
in the deep dark seas
of an illicit three way love affair.
Giant Jupiter Jack,
naked and laughing
with two beautiful women
fawning over my soul at the same time.
On a clever California coastline.
poet prophet me,
kissing and being kissed
stroking and being stroked
into the oblivion of humanity's lost divinity,
which is a lack of inhibition
possessed by a child in waiting.
Right now I am a god,
a minor deity of my own religion…
being made holy
by kisses.

SHE MOVES IN MAGIC

She smells like Sunday school,
walking along sunshine side walks
of the golden California afternoon.
I dally behind her
memorizing the scent of her hair
as it mixes with jasmine
from heaven's own heart.
It is beyond me
to understand how she moves in magic,
in madness, in mystery...
in me.

FOREVER IN HER

I am a saint
by the sentience of her touch,
in her smile
is all the salvation in the world…
forgiveness in a kiss
hope in a hand
forever
in her.

WALKING IN BEAUTY

She floats like prayer,
lonely on her pilgrimage to heaven…
rising incense making its way to God,
I worship her in the silence
of a full moon shining from her eyes.
I am a stranger in her smile
these starry distant shores
of the never ending now
have convinced me of the obvious.
Truth is a woman
walking in beauty.

IT'S OUR FAULT

We don't know when too much is too much,
and when enough is enough,
because we let too many things get in the way
of the possibility of Us.
Our poetry is being lost in the screams…
lost in the goodbyes
lost in the inevitable madness of
"it's your fault, it's my fault"
when the truth is, it's our fault
and no one else's.
It's our fault that we let our sanity
slip through the cracks of our joy,
it's our fault that we can't let go of the sins
that keep us in the darkness,
it's our fault that
we are the children of drama
and feel the need to keep being born,
it's our fault for all the sleepless nights
all the tormented days
and all the bitter blame games
played at the expense of each other…
it's our fault and no one else's,
but I guess it's my fault
for writing it down.

I WILL NEVER FORGET

Last night I was reborn
from your womb of tears and trust…
dripping wet like a
bubble of destruction and hope.
That's what you called me
in a moment of true love…
as we struggle of make amends
for all the miserable sins
committed against each other
in the madness of our lives.
I kiss you where it hurts,
but the pain may never go away.
You are my midnight
and in you is all the moon
I will ever need.
You are my noonday
and in you is all the sun I can bear.
You are my tragedy
and in you is all the remembrance
I will never forget.

THE COINCIDENCE OF BECOMING

Watching you
is like staring into the sun,
I go blind
in the beauty of your bounce...
from the moment we said hello
I had the sensation
that I had suddenly jumped off a cliff
and was falling imminently towards heaven...
up instead of down,
no gravity,
just you and I
getting lost in the clouds of our hello...
like angels stumbling over wings
not knowing what to do with them,
accidentally learning to fly
by the coincidence of becoming.

SUDDEN RUSH

...and manna never tasted so good
as your kiss...
heaven has nothing near as sweet
as you on a summer day,
glowing rune of my desire
containing ancient wisdom in your breasts
disguised as milk...
I am a pilgrim
in the journey of your soul,
I glide through you
like children at play
in the kingdom of innocence
all is sudden rush
when I'm with you.

NEVER FORGOTTEN

Ahhhh the moon…
the most tragic face of all,
like an explosion in the sky
telling the story of infinite sadness.
She weeps for you as a glowing saint of eternity…
reminding you of what you've lost
~your divinity~
"godling…" she says,
"Remember you are a child of mine…come home."
And we smile and we point,
and wonder why the moon is so alone in the night.
She is our mother,
Earth is her womb,
we are lost without her smile.
We are orphans remembering,
always remembering
but never forgotten.

A THING OF POETRY

There is no shame in you…
your breasts contain the universe.
In one, all the madness in the world,
in the other, infinite sadness.
Your womb is an explosion,
being born forever.
You are God's prayer to femininity,
soft, subtle, sweet as rain.
I am a poet lost in remembrance of you,
even as you are
I am reminded of what you were,
and what you will always be…
the stature of my desire,
a saint of men's dreams
a child of laughter…
giggling uncontrollably
for all to see,
a thing of poetry.

MY POEM

I love you without knowing why
or how…or where it comes from.
I love you completely
and without measure…
I love you like the ocean loves the sand
and so sends wave kisses to greet the earth…
I love you beyond myself,
in spite of myself
more than myself…
You are the beauty of the universe
in the form of a woman,
more peace in your eyes
than all the poems can tell…
more possibility in your smile
than every star in the sky…
more hope in your soul
than I have words to describe.
In your absence I can barely breathe
I am broken without you…
know only pain without you
my sky
my beloved
my poem.

MY FUTURE

When god created the moon and the stars
IT hadn't yet imagined
the beauty that would become you...
if IT had, then there would be no earth,
no heaven...only you dwelling in perfect beauty.
After you there is nothing,
before you there is nothing...
beyond you there is only imperfection.
In you is all the heaven I will ever need,
when we were still atoms in the mind of God...
I met you, loved you,
and have been searching for you ever since.
And now that I have found you...
I am once again complete.
I see in you
all my tomorrows,
all my hopeful longings at peace...
all my desires fulfilled.
I live to be with you,
die to be without you...
know only you,
my angel,
my Goddess,
my future.

AN ARTIST IN LOVE

I sketch you with these words
like an artist in love...
You have been drawn on my heart forever.

ALWAYS

You brush your teeth
like prayer in the morning…
politely…in soft easy motions,
everything you do is like worship…
I watch you from the quiet birth of dawn
and think of you as a godling,
discovering its divinity…
I have loved you always.

THE POSSIBILITY OF US

You are God's poem to beauty…
IT wrote you on a canvas of perfection and respect,
Your name sounds like dignity on my tongue,
When I speak it…
All the universe pauses for prayer.
How holy you must be as you dwell in time…
Like a thing to be honored.
Let me be your completion…
Take me by the hand
As you so often take me by the eye,
Knowing my soul without the need for words
Only the sentience of our stare.
I asked god for a moment of laughter…
And he gave me a universe of happiness in you.
Never has there been
Nor will there ever be
A truth more profound
Than the one which can be found
In the possibility of us.

THE GODHOOD I DISCOVERED IN YOU

Sometimes I see you in purple…
sometimes I see you in green…
and sometimes…
when I'm living an almost unbearably normal moment,
like staring blankly into the distance,
at the nothing that comprises my time…
I think of you,
and my day becomes a little more spectacular…
you are the richest jewel in my treasure of thoughts
shining like a serpentine scepter
in a sea of detritus and inconsequence,
reminding me of my divinity,
my good fortune
the godhood I discovered in you.

KISSNAPPED

I couldn't sleep last night…
I kept thinking about your skin and the way it
curves on my tongue.
Like it did yesterday
as we lay hidden, tangled
among sheets and towels
in the back of my jeep…
hung sloppily to conceal our madness!
With only 3 hours to spare
we decided to exchange naked kisses
in the L.A.X. short term parking.
Your breath smelled sweet
like babies do after they've eaten apple sauce,
I memorized you there,
all of you
like a map to the most important
decision of my entire life…
I memorized each curve,
each smell,
each fleeting word
and the delicate sounds they made as they
fell on my ears…
And as cramped as we were…
I have never been so comfortable with anybody,
I wanted to kissnapp you,
steal you away with my lips,
make Taiwan seem like a field trip
in comparison to the places I would take you
in the poetry of our togetherness.
I wanted you to let go of everything

and just dwell with me
in perfect beauty…
in laughter and in silence,
I wanted…
I want still.

I Don't Mind Bleeding

I do not doubt that she loved me,
but always with that sort of vague look of mistrust
which comes from the corner of the eye
and suspects the worst.
I was never half as bad as she imagined,
but only twice as determined
to keep something to myself.
It's funny how secrets eventually become lies
if there not told in due time.
But how do you tell jealously
that you have a friend?
She will kill every strand of kindness
to do away with that connection.
I have lost so much in loving her
and now I find myself back here,
in the familiar place of poetry,
that is tormenting me to write it all down…
she'll no doubt read this one day
and sigh sarcastically
but that will not diminish the truth of it…
she was a thorn
that I bore
just to smell the rose,
and as much as I bled from her sting,
it was worth it
to know her soul.
I carry her now inside me
like a wound that will not heal,

but I don't mind bleeding
in honor of love.

UNTIL THE DARKNESS

She is the only person I know
who can insult me
and compliment me at the same time…
in that wicked sort of way
that belies all resentful lovers.
Still, she was my better half for a while…
until the darkness
prevented her from bearing a grin,
she used to smile to see me…
and when that disappeared
so did we.

WHICH ONE I LIKE MORE

She is an instrument and a weapon,
sometimes I play her strings with my tongue
and she writhes with pleasure and moans…
it sounds just like music.
And sometimes she stabs me with words
like a warrior intent on the kill…
with whoops and yells
screaming for revenge!
When we're at odds
there is no hope!
But when we're at peace
all the world is soft
there is no fear…
or loathing,
only kindness and kisses.
I can't decide
which one I like more.

EMERALD

She said her name was emerald…
And sure enough,
she looked like a jewel to me…
smiling her way into the room like some sort of lost angel
searching for the divinity she once knew…
I felt like a myth flying too close to the sun,
because in her smile,
was all the kindness in the world.
I like to think of her as a dream I had
on some lonesome summer day
that I'll remember from time to time
to make myself smile.
People will see me grinning
and wonder what sort of nectar I've tasted…
I'll tell them it was the essence of compassion and mercy
in the form of a woman I didn't really know,
but felt connected to in faith,
a treasure,
a jewel
Emerald.

THE NIRVANA OF SKIN

Your kiss is my favorite candy…
I am unraveled in your eyes
like a child in the presence of magic.
We stare…and everything becomes a chocolate sea of delights
eatable in every sense of the word.
I wish I could share you with the world
so that the universe might know the taste of heaven's own heart.
You dwell in sweet serenity
of the never ending now,
your scent is the secret that I keep hidden in my heart's hideaway
like a truth that could change the world
if only it weren't so fragile…
to speak it would mean its demise
and with it the loss of maybe.
And so I tuck you away
along with all memorable moments
of stolen beauty that I have acquired along this journey…
I keep your smile as a token of what passion looks like
when its been tickled to the point of enlightenment.
Because you remind me of why I was created
to be a poet in love with poetry
making music in the name of muses…
to kiss, to love, to live
and not simply exist.
Your touch has replaced all my religion
as the most holy of experiences,
by you I am made mysteriously matriarchal,
my sensibility severely severed from my soul
until all I know
is the nirvana of skin

found in your cheek
dripping from your neck
like golden prayers
of the eternal scripture.

I HAVE A SECRET

"I have a secret…" says he poetically.
"What?" she asks softly.
"My lips are falling in love with you." says he.
They kiss and the world disappears in the wet of skin and breath…
"I have another secret…" says he.
"What?" she asks again in anticipation.
"My tongue is falling in love with you too…" says he.
They smile and laugh the secret laugh of lovers lost in each other,
and all the night is blessed by their holiness.
They become so entangled
that at times its hard to tell the difference between them
and which soul belongs in whose body,
until at length…all they can do is radiate beauty
like an oracle of new beginnings.
"What if I told you I love you?" asks he.
"I love you too…" she says with sincerity…
"What if I told you I was falling IN love with you?" asks he.
"Then I'd say…tell your lips and your tongue
that mine feel the same…."
she says with complete kindness.
He holds her close to himself
like a promise being kept,
and together the are quiet in the night
with nowhere to be
except in each other's arms…
which is where all legends begin
on the cusp of risk
and in a moment

of complete and utter connectedness
like this one, forbidden, mad, happening.

I WONDER WHAT YOU'D SAY?

If I could tell you anything…
it would be that some part of you
inhabits me in your absence,
not in a profound way…
but subtle, like a whisper in the memory of my soul
reminding me of beauty,
reminding me of God's poetry…
reminding me of what the dawning of existence must have looked like.
It's in the way you smile
moving like a cloud in the epiphany of my mind,
it's in the way you smell…
faintly sweet as you pass my way,
it's in the way you laugh
like a child at play,
with out care or concern for anything except the magic of moonlight.
If I could tell you anything
it would be that from the moment I saw you…
I memorized your smile
like I would a poem that I admired,
I did it because in a world of ugliness
I needed something beautiful to take me away…
I did it because of the mystery that is you,
I did it because I'm a sentimental romantic poet,
because I am a man
and you are a woman…
I did it because I didn't know what else to do
with the suddenness of your appearance.
If I could tell you anything
it would be that I never intended to give you this…
I never knew that I'd have the courage,

never thought you wouldn't feel harassed or awkward,
and I never knew until now
that I could share this with you
without expecting anything in return.
If I could tell you anything it would be this
that you remind me of someone I never knew
but always hoped I'd meet,
I'd say that I can no more be held responsible for my thoughts
than you can be for your beauty…
I'd ask you to forgive me for not saying this before
and then I'd ask you to forget that I ever said anything in the first place,
because I'd rather you forget than be anything but what you are
a divine expression of God's smile…
I'd tell you that I meant no harm,
but only found you worthy of praise…
I'd ask you to not let this become uncomfortable
but to be insightful enough to take it for what it is…
a silly little poem about beauty.
I'd tell you all of this,
and then I'd smile and walk away.
I wonder what you'd say?

SO MUCH TO ASK

I wanna' tell you something
that I've never told another soul...
I want it to be something
that no one has every told you either,
something you never expected to hear
from another human being as long as you lived...
I want it to change your life
like only truth can,
in a way that is profound and forever...
I want you to weep when you hear it,
tears of complete and utter enlightenment
born from the tear duct of God's own eye...
I want you to feel every cell in your body come alive with
Peruvian delight as my words make love to your heart
with such delicate poetry....
that you are sure you'll lay in them
every night before you sleep.
I wanna' be that secret that you tell your children
when they ask you about all the crazy things you did when you were young,
I want you to think of me then
and smile the crooked smile
of unforgettable blazing nights spent in the presence of divinity.
I want all our moments to be alive
and saturated with something unspeakable
like the stuff of stars and magic
innocent child dreams
bursting from the mind of milk fed toddlers
whose only world is their mothers breasts.
I want to become such a part of your life
that when you come to die

you discover that we are inseparable
like the drops of rain that mingle with the river
and so become a part of all that is
flowing wild from heaven to earth
in a strenuous effort to find a home.
I wanna' remind you that there isn't a thing in the universe
that you can have or do
if you only believe in the power of what it means to exist...
I wanna' be the example you follow
when you're thinking of doing something
completely impractical and absurd.
I wanna' have you hear your friends or loved ones say
"That's impossible...you're crazy!"
and then think to your self...
well if he did it
then maybe I can too.
I want you to remember that I was a poet
a prophet, a madman, a real person
much like yourself
just trying to find my way in this world.
I want you to remember that I stumbled a lot along the way
but that I never stopped,
never gave up
never quit believing
that there is something bigger than all of this
meaningless garbage called normalcy
that we fill our lives with
in an effort to forget...
I want you to say my name with conviction
with anger
with love
with something other than a passing fancy

and when you do
I want you to feel
that you've been affected somehow by
the madness that is me.
I want this and everything else possibility has to offer
is that so much to ask?

SENTIENT AND ALWAYS

...and now, all my religion is in you,
I worship your beauty with palm to palm kisses
of "I once was lost
but now am found" in your eyes
of forgiveness without knowing.
In you I have become reborn
a thing of divinity
sprung from the most holy of moments
which is you and I under cover of night and moon
making our music with breath and skin.
If there was ever any sin in me
it was in the desire I felt for the possibility of us
to become like gods in our own right...
soaring on the un-nameable substance called being in love.
I have abandoned all my idolatry
and in its place
set up the graven image of you
which burns quietly in my heart's sanctuary.
Someone once asked me who made God...
I had no answer,
but now I think that God must have come from
the uncontrollable desire of existence to be in love
and in that creation
was found the completion of all that is...
from a moment such as this
we too were born
like golden eternities
overflowing with the wisdom of touch...
We dwell now,
as the untouchable essence

that is felt in every kiss of true love,
and therein we remain
sentient and always.

WITHOUT THE NEED FOR WORDS

We watched the candlelight dance
with shadows on the ceiling,
as we lay naked and spent
from our most recent passion.
I can barely contain myself
as the press of your skin on mine
unfolds my desire like hope waiting to be worn.
Long stares of silent grinning saints
as we contemplate the implications of each other's souls,
and what it means to touch the tenderest threads of youth.
There is an ancient sound playing in the background,
playing like prophecy as we mingle in the arms of heaven…
I am reminded of what it was like when I was eight,
and all the world seemed new and alive…
I convinced of what it will be like when I am eighty
if I were with someone like you,
someone who exists as a constant reminder
of tenderness and compassion.
Someone whose heart is a reflection of God's own heart,
and whose touch feels like promise,
more than promise,
like poetry…
being spoken without the need for words,
but in complete and utter understanding.
In long drawn out breaths of
I love you, and forever.

YOU AND I

We took a drive down hope street,
and watched the skyscrapers dance with the wind.
Just two brothers dwelling in poetry
like gurus of tomorrow's hopeful becoming.
The hum of wheels…top down,
and the California summer night to guide our way
as we contemplate the enormity of being.
I remember when you were just beginning to write
and you'd let me look over your poems
like a veteran warrior looking at weapons.
We'd discuss the importance of changing the world
and falling in love…
I miss that most of all,
the discussions that began with a brawl
and ended with poems.
Suddenly we were in different places,
different places in our lives
different places in our minds
different.
Yet somehow, through it all
the Us in We remained unchanged…
and now when I think of what it means to be a madman prophet…
to scream like a loon
to be in love with the mistake of life,
I think of you and I
making our way in the world
without the aid of sanity…
I think of all the poems we've written since the beginning
and all the ones we'll write from now on…
I think of the sleeping poets

all across the world
who are waiting to be waken up
from their death of normalcy...
I think of God and enlightenment,
I think of you and I.

ME TOO

It's midnight again
and we are playing in the back of my Jeep
like two lost children
in search of innocence.
Our secret silence turns to kisses
which turns to loving laughter,
which ends in forbidden hidden poetry…
And all the while
I am staring into your eyes
wondering "how lucky can I really be?
That such beauty has been placed in my path
like a truth waiting to be found."
It's cold outside
and so we hold each other close
in the car that we call a shrine,
because we have no where else to be
except in the arms of our illegitimate love.
Quietly I slip inside you
and listen to the sound of your breath
as it makes me believe
that I am truly alive.
Whispered I love you's
tender wet kisses,
and heart beats…
like becoming.
My only hope
is in being your puppet,
letting you play with the strings of my soul
making me dance with delight
from having known your womb.

Even now,
while you are miles away
in a place where I am not welcome
among friends who don't know me
and wouldn't approve if they did…
I am hidden within your belly,
I deposited myself there last night
while we were making love under a crescent-moon
that was big in the sky.
It looked like God falling asleep,
while we clung to the divinity of our youth…
I remember saying that "I could be in you forever"
you smiled and said
"me too…"

PANIC

You just left suddenly,
in the middle of our song
and I got this sad sense of goodbye…
everyone was watching
so I pretended to not care,
but inside I am dying.
My hands keep asking me
where you are so they can touch you again…
I tell them you'll be back soon
but they don't believe me,
neither does my lips
whose only prayer to me
is that they kiss you again.
My soul keeps assuring me
that if you do not return soon
it will surely leave me
in search of you again…
I tried to remain calm
but panic is the name of this poem
and it is murdering my thoughts
even as I speak.
I know you love me…
I just can't remember why.

SANCTUARY

Sleep well my sweet,
for as long as I live,
nothing shall hurt you tonight.
You will dream in perfect serenity…
as I stand watchful by the midnight door.
All that threatens you
has been silenced,
all that seeks you out has been deterred.
All that is left,
are your smiles being reborn as laughter.
You are a grinning saint,
and my arms have become your shrine.
There is sanctuary here,
and deep breaths of longing…
my eyes are an altar,
set in unblinking prayer over you.
I hold you now as I do my own soul,
with complete regard,
and sanctimonious possession…
like a treasure that I must safe-guard
until I am called away into the unceasing night…
where I will take you like a memory
to be fastened to the stars.
Forgive me for my many many faults
they were the blemishes of passion
that bound me to you.
I am connected to you
even after the last syllable of time,
and then I will tie myself to you
when there is no more.

All that I am,
all that I have been,
and all that I shall become
belongs to you.
And so, sleep well my sweet,
for as long as I live,
nothing shall hurt you tonight
nor any other.

END TO BEGIN

It's only after we've lost everything that we can truly appreciate anything...

In losing you I have remembered why I found you in the first place.

Somewhere in those watery eyes

I see my truest friend crying goodbye...

and so if we must cease to be,

let us do so in memory of who we once were together...

Let us say goodbye with longing,

and understanding, and a kind touch...

Let us remember every single moment good and bad,

as the story we wrote together...

and in so doing,

let us keep in mind that we alone have the power to end this story...

and it can end any way we chose.

So, let it be an ending unlike any other,

an ending that completes and defies itself at the same time...

an ending that is in actuality a beginning.

Let us find ourselves hiding among the remnants of our shattered hearts,

And let us be put back together as different creatures.

It's only after we've lost everything that we can truly appreciate anything...

Together as we are reborn separately,

let us hold a quiet vigil for our lost selves,

the fractured personalities that will always be searching for each other in the Martian night.

Let us write a new beginning,

one that doesn't begin with a kiss...

one where no one has to be ashamed of who they are,

one that begins with a laugh,

and evolves into a behavior seldom seen in this sad mad world.

It's only after we've lost everything that we can truly appreciate anything...

Let us be the authors of this new child called Poetry,

And may this new born universe find its purpose in non-judgment.

May it be made of forgiveness and shine,

may its heart beat with hope,

may it bring us some comfort and enlightenment to know

that we let go with our dignities still in tact.

Stay in my life as a permanent guest,

And never ask me to leave the porthole of your soul either.

Let us be the poems that we each write with permanent ink…

The kind we cannot forget because they speak to us in the silence and the absence.

I have etched your name here forever,

and I see my own name still thriving in you too…

and in this way we end,

And in this way we begin.

0-595-30384-6

LaVergne, TN USA
23 August 2009
155651LV00006B/63/A